EULOGY
OF
JUDGES

Written by a Lawyer
PIERO CALAMANDREI

Translated by John Clarke Adams
and C. Abbott Phillips, Jr.

With a New Preface by
Jacob A. Stein

THE LAWBOOK EXCHANGE, LTD.
Clark, New Jersey

ISBN 978-1-58477-760-1 (hardcover)
ISBN 978-1-58477-902-5 (paperback)

Lawbook Exchange edition 2006, 2011

Printed by arrangement with Princeton University Press

Printed in the United States of America on acid-free paper

THE LAWBOOK EXCHANGE, LTD.
33 Terminal Avenue
Clark, New Jersey 07066-1321

*Please see our website for a selection of our other publications
and fine facsimile reprints of classic works of legal history:*
www.lawbookexchange.com

Library of Congress Cataloging-in-Publication Data

Calamandrei, Piero, 1889-1956.
  [Elogio dei giudici. English]
  Euology of judges / author, Piero Calamandrei ; translated by John Clarke Adams and C. Abbott Phillips, Jr. ; Jacob A. Stein, author of new preface.
      p. cm.
  Translation of: Elogio dei giudici.
  Originally published: Princeton, N.J. : Princeton University Press, c1942.
    ISBN-13: 978-1-58477-760-1 (cloth : alk. paper)
    ISBN-10: 1-58477-760-5 (cloth : alk. paper)
  1. Judges. 2. Lawyers. I. Title.

  K2146.C3513 2006
  347'.014--dc22   2006026487

A Lawyer's Preface
to the New Edition of
The Eulogy for Judges

Those of us who are members of the Piero Calamandrei freemasonry society agree, without dissent, that *Eulogy of Judges* is the best lawyer's book ever written. I came across the *Eulogy* fifty years ago. I was struck by its doubly distilled offering up of what a lawyer learns from years of dealing with clients, judges, and the courts.

Calamandrei tells us that we have been given the right to study human imperfection, its inconsistent hopes and fears. That is why we suppress the impulse to ask a client why he lied when he knew he would be caught. Why he risked the necessary in order to get the superfluous? Why does he want to sue his own brother?

Calamandrei is aware that it is not the great events such as swimming the Hellespont that teach us what we need to know. It is the small things, the daily round of the butcher, the baker and the candlestick maker. It is, as William Blake said:

> To see a world in a grain of sand
> And a heaven in a wild flower,
> Hold infinity in the palm of your hand
> And eternity in an hour

Reading Calamandrei is like reading Proust's *Remembrance of Things Past*, Gogol's *The Overcoat* and Thomas Mann's *The Confessions of Felix Krull*. These are books in which we discover what lies hidden between the lines.

Despite the fact that Calamandrei's practice was confined to the Italian legal system, it is apparent that what he describes is the same where people find reasons to disagree with each other. That is to say everywhere. The biases and prejudices of witnesses, the greed of clients, the logorrheatic lawyers and the weary judges are on display for all to see wherever we may roam.

I assume that the courts where Mr. Calamandrei practiced were not perfect. No doubt they were subject to the same cynical gossip that can be heard in some of our own big city courts. Mr. Calamandrei dispels this cynicism by an ironical ambush:

> If a lawyer enters the courtroom armed with subterfuge and clever dialectics, if he relies upon the partiality of the judges or their corruptibility instead of relying upon honest argument, he should not be surprised to find himself not in an austere temple of justice but rather in a hall of mirrors like those one finds at fairs, where from every wall his intrigues return to him multiplied and distorted. To find purity in the courtroom, one must enter with a pure heart. Even here what Father Christopher said applies: "Omniamunde mundis." All things are pure to the pure in heart. (p.3)

In another passage Mr. Calamandrei describes a joyful experience that every lawyer has had who assumes the worst when he is a stranger in a strange courthouse.

> You are exhausted and discouraged. Failure seems inevitable. Bitterly you repeat to your-

self that you can hope for nothing from the court. And then when the decision is handed down, you hear that you have won, despite your inferiority, the eloquence of your adversary, the dreaded friendships and the vaunted protection. These are a lawyer's red-letter days, when he learns that against every expedient of art or intrigue he can win with justice on his side. (p.4)

I had such an experience. I learned the hard way that I should never seek justice in a faraway court where I knew no one. I broke that resolution in order to represent a friend. However I had prepared myself and my friend for an adverse ruling. I was ready for what has been called home cooking. Despite all our apprehensions, we won. The judge treated me as any other lawyer in his court, known and unknown. He ruled against my opponent, the local fixer. It was, as Calamandrei said, one of my red letter days.

Calamandrei's gift for irony is demonstrated again in chapter 5, entitled *On a Certain Immobility of Judges on the Bench*. He sides with the judge who falls asleep during a lawyer's presentation of the merits of his client's case. He says that there are tactics a judge may employ to deal with a lawyer who insists on talking when he has nothing to say. The judge can tell the lawyer to sit down and shut-up. The judge can interrupt the lawyer with questions that demonstrate what is being said misses the point. But for Calamandrei the best tactic is for the judge simply to take a nap. "I believe that many times judges' sleep is premeditated. It is a voluntary procedure which relieves them of the burden of hearing what a lawyer has to say and still permits them to decide the case in favor of his client on their own grounds."

I have seen a judge fall asleep at a bench conference that went on too long. I have seen a judge fall asleep and fall backwards out of his chair as the lawyer at the podium kept on talking. I have seen judges who have an agreement with the courtroom clerk to sound an alarm by dropping *Black's Law Dictionary* on the floor when the clerk sees the judge nod off.

I know of a case that went to the Court of Appeals on the issue that the trial judge fell asleep during part of a witness's testimony. The Court of Appeals in its opinion ruled that the appellant failed to show that the testimony, when it was contended the judge was dozing, was testimony that was not crucial to the issues.

Calamandrei likes to see a judge doze off when he, Calamandrei, is speaking. "Sleep is the most discreet method which the judge has at his command for quietly tiptoeing away when what I have to say no longer interests him, thus leaving me to talk to myself in peace."

Calamandrei devotes a chapter to *On Litigiousness*. "The honest lawyer should be more than a clinician of the legal profession, he should be a hygienist as well. Considering their daily work of disinfecting litigious persons, relieving the courtrooms of their disputes, judges should realize that lawyers, after all are their most faithful collaborators." Calamandrei quotes a sage who says the age of 60 is the best age for litigiousness. In Calamandrei's experience (and mine) there are people of all ages stricken with the litigation disease.

He says he knew a litigant more than ninety years old, who after the age of sixty brought a suit over a disputed inheritance. His young adversaries decided that the best tactic was to wear the old man out by delay in order to hasten his death, which they expected in the near future. Thus began an epic duel between civil procedure and longevity. As the years passed, generations of lawyers defended the parties. One by one the judges who handed down the early decisions went to their last rest. The old gentleman, instead of aging, took on new life from every procedural objection which postponed the final decision. With his patriarchal beard flying over pockets full of pleadings, he went on against his adversaries who felt they were bringing on his death by their procrastination. Little did they realize that only victory would kill him.

Litigiousness, like love, is a talkative passion. Mr. Litigious cannot escape from his circle of suspicions. He goes on and on about the schemes of others, the mistreatment he has suffered, mental and physical, heavy damages, the need for damages, compensatory and punitive damages, the need for an injunction and an award of attorneys' fees. He has been to other lawyers. He wants to sue the lawyers who filed one of his cases after the limitation statutes had run. He has folders filled with letters with the envelopes attached. I have discovered that the way for me to disengage from such a person is to detach the envelopes from the letters as I say that envelopes needlessly clutter a file. I toss the envelopes in the trash basket. Mr. Litigious immediately retrieves the envelopes. He must have them to prove the letters were sent so that the sender cannot say the letters were never sent. I am now in his ring of suspicion. He quickly departs.

Calamandrei uses a delightful metaphor to explain the relationship between the lawyers and the Judge. He says that a London gallery has a painting showing Cardinal Richelieu in three different poses. In the center is the Cardinal in full face. On each side is the Cardinal in profile, each facing the full face portrait. "It is the same with a law suit. The lawyers present the two profiles of truth, but only the judge in the center looks it full in the face."

Calamandrei did not like to let go of the metaphor. "Place two painters side by side before the same landscape, each with his own easel, and return an hour or so later to see what each has on his canvas. You will find two landscapes so different that it will seem impossible that they were drawn from the same model.

"Would you say that one of the artists has betrayed the truth?"

I could go on but it is time to call upon the guest of honor to tell us what this practice of law is all about. Ladies and gentlemen, here is, in person, the Master of advocacy, Piero Calamandrei.

I will close now so that you can see for yourself how lucky you are to have this book in hand.

Jacob A. Stein
Washington, D.C.
August 2006

EULOGY
OF
JUDGES

Written by a Lawyer
PIERO CALAMANDREI
Translated by John Clarke Adams
and C. Abbott Phillips, Jr.

Published by Princeton University
Press, at Princeton, New Jersey, in
Nineteen hundred forty-six

PRINTED IN THE UNITED STATES OF AMERICA
BY PRINCETON UNIVERSITY PRESS AT PRINCETON, NEW JERSEY
LONDON: GEOFFREY CUMBERLEGE, OXFORD UNIVERSITY PRESS

to Franco
WHO MATRICULATED
IN LAW
1935

TRANSLATORS' PREFACE

IT is the good fortune of most students to meet in the course of their academic progression from grammar school to the more advanced and esoteric realms of knowledge, one or two, or perhaps, if they are very lucky, several great teachers who inspire them to an increased love of knowledge and who endow them with a deeper understanding of humanity.

Such an experience befell one of the translators when he attended the lectures of Piero Calamandrei. Neither previous acquaintance with the man nor previous interest in the subject matter prompted this young American college graduate to study the elements of Italian civil procedure at the University of Florence. The course was chosen for the fortuitous circumstance that Professor Calamandrei was clean shaven, a fact of considerable importance to a foreigner whose knowledge of Italian was so limited that he needed to watch lips as well as listen to sounds in his effort to understand. After the first weeks, however, the course ceased to serve merely as an Italian lesson for the American visitor and became one of the most stimulating and memorable series of lectures which he has been privileged to attend. There are those who say that civil procedure is as dull a subject as can be found in any curriculum. In Florence, at least, this is not so, for Piero Calamandrei has a vocation for the law and for teaching. He opened before his students the vast field of legal theory and as he explained court procedure to them he filled them with a reverence for the bar and made them share with him the faith that there is no higher calling than that of a champion of justice.

It would be unfair to Professor Calamandrei's varied

talents if he were to be depicted merely as a lawyer and a teacher. His rank as a leading scholar in his field is attested to by his *Studi sul processo civile*, a series of essays on problems of procedure and phases of legal theory which runs into many volumes. His interest in legal history has led him to compile an amusing volume of anecdotes on bench and bar. At other times he has fared even further afield and published volumes of verse. His proficiency in the arts, however, is not confined to poetry, for he is an accomplished painter who has done among other things the charming illustrations which adorn the Italian edition of the present work, and his interest in music has made him prominent among the Florentine patrons of that muse. In short, Piero Calamandrei is a living example of the distinguished tradition of the Tuscan Renaissance, whose leaders never permitted a profound study of their particular fields of endeavor to take from them their highest distinction: a catholicity of interest and a humanistic approach which made these scholars and artists gentlemen as well.

The present book, the first of his works to appear in English, was published in 1936 and has since appeared in a second enlarged Italian edition, as well as a French translation. The present translation is based on the second Italian edition.

JOHN CLARKE ADAMS
C. ABBOTT PHILLIPS, JR.

CONTENTS

EULOGY OF JUDGES

CHAPTER I

On Faith in Judges, The Prime Requisite of a Lawyer

WHO was it that invented that cowardly and temporizing proverb, *Habent sua sidera lites*? Though couched in decorous Latin it says in effect that justice is a game of chance, never to be taken seriously. Surely the expression was coined by some legal hireling without scruples or passion, hoping in some way to excuse his own incompetence, to overcome his remorse, and to lessen his toil. But you, young lawyer, cast aside this epigram of resignation, this enervating drug; burn the page where it is written, and when you take a case that seems just, work fervently with the conviction that by faith in justice you will succeed in changing the course of the stars, regardless of the astrologers.

❖

HE who seeks justice must believe in justice, who like all divinities, shows her face only to the faithful.

❖

IF a lawyer enters the courtroom armed with subterfuge and clever dialectics, if he relies upon the partiality of the judges or their corruptibility instead of relying upon honest argument, he should not be surprised to find himself not in an austere temple of justice but rather in a hall of mirrors like those one finds at fairs, where from every wall his intrigues return to him multiplied and distorted. To find purity in the courtroom, one must enter with a pure heart. Even here what Father Christopher said applies: "*Omnia munda mundis.*"[1]

✧

You are pleading an important case, one of those cases which are not rare even in the private law field, a case where a man's life or the happiness of a family depends on the outcome. You are convinced that your client is in the right. Not only has he the law on his side but the moral conviction of society, which is far more important. You know that you must win if justice is to prevail, but you are full of doubts and fears. Your adversary is more learned, more eloquent, and has greater prestige than you have. His briefs are composed with a subtlety you do not possess; the presiding judge is his personal friend; the judges consider him a master, and you know there are powerful interests behind his client. On the day of the trial you are sure you have argued badly, that you have overlooked your strongest points and have wearied the judges, who were wreathed in smiles at the brilliant defense of your opponent.

You are exhausted and discouraged. Failure seems inevitable. Bitterly you repeat to yourself that you can hope for nothing from the court. And then, when the decision is handed down, you hear that you have won, despite your inferiority, the eloquence of your adversary, the dreaded friendships and the vaunted protection. These are a lawyer's red-letter days, when he learns that against every expedient of art or intrigue he can win with justice on his side.

✧

THE modest lawyer, even the beginner, should not be alarmed to find himself facing one of those so-called

---

[1] "All things are pure to the pure in heart."

Princes of the Forum, a man distinguished by his learning, his eloquence, his political influence, or perhaps only by the airs he gives himself. If the young lawyer is convinced that he is defending a just cause, and if he knows how to present his case simply and clearly, he will learn that where the powers of the opposing attorneys are unequal, the judges are generally disposed to bestow their admiration on the more brilliant and to give their protection to the least talented.

❖

OFTENTIMES, through that common desire to protect the weak against the strong, the judges unconsciously tend to favor the party who is less ably defended. If he finds a judge with a generous heart, an inexpert lawyer can bring success to his client.

❖

IF your adversary is known for his sharp practices, do not try to compete with him in setting traps. Frankly admit your inferiority at playing his game and show the court that you will oppose his cunning with a simple faith in justice.

Usually I have won my case against attorneys more "clever" than I, and when I lost I was proud not to be in the place of the victor.

❖

IN his *Ricordi* Guicciardini crudely observes that, in spite of all the procedural precautions the jurists have devised to reduce the chance of a miscarriage of justice, half of the decisions are still erroneous. This would mean that our judgments are no better than the decisions of the Turkish judges, which, as legend has it, were determined by lot. His implication would seem to be that all the effort expended by civilized peoples to perfect the judicial process has been thrown to the winds, and that instead of deluding ourselves with the hope that our poor logic may ever succeed in finding justice, we might better follow the example of Rabelais' good judge who, in order to be perfectly impartial, decided each case with a throw of the dice.

It is clear that holding this disconsolate conviction Guicciardini was not fitted for the bar, where cold hearts are not wanted, and that he did well to change his profession while still a young man. But he who has a vocation for the law will tell you that, even if all the labor that modern civilization has dedicated to its perfection has only raised the number of just decisions one per cent, this work would not have been in vain; even if all the efforts of the judges and lawyers to discern the light of truth through the mist were futile, even if not the slightest tangible result were gained thereby, theirs would still be a holy work, perhaps the highest expression of that spirit which distinguishes man from beast. The desperate effort of him who seeks truth is never fruitless, even though his thirst remains unquenched. Blessed are they that hunger and thirst for justice.

❖

THERE are times in the career of every lawyer when, forgetting the niceties of the codes, the arts of oratory, the technique of debating, unconscious of his robes or those of the judges, he turns to the judges, looking into their eyes as into the eyes of an equal, and speaks to them in the simple words a man uses to convince his fellow man of the truth. In these moments justice is reborn and he who pronounces the word feels a suppliant tremor in his voice like that in the prayers of the faithful.

These moments of humble and solemn sincerity repay the lawyer for all his labor.

✧

THE aphorism of the scholars, *Res iudicata facit de albo nigrum et de quadrato rotundum,*[2] makes us laugh today, but if we were more thoughtful it might disturb us not a little. The judge, like the wizard of the fairy story, has the power to make the most monstrous metamorphosis in the world of law and to give to shadows the eternal appearance of substance. Since in his world decision and truth should coincide, he can by an incorrect decision reduce truth to the measure of his ability.

With an eloquence no jurist has equaled, Socrates serenely demonstrated to his disciples that supreme social rule which imposes obedience to legal decisions, even unto the extreme sacrifice, and even though they may be unjust. The final judgment of a case is dissociated from its motivation, as the butterfly which has left its cocoon, and it can no longer be classified as just or unjust, as it is now destined to constitute the final and immutable statement to which man turns to know the official word of justice.

For this reason the state feels the importance of the selection of judges; for it knows it is entrusting to them the dangerous power which, when abused, makes injustice just, forces the majesty of the law to serve evil, and indelibly marks white-robed innocence with a bloody brand which makes her indistinguishable from guilt.

✧

So long as the law is not disturbed, it surrounds us as invisibly and impalpably as the air we breathe, as un-

---

2 "The judgments of courts can turn white into black and square into round."

noticed as the health we appreciate only after it is lost. But when the law is threatened and abused, descending from the astral world where it reposed as a hypothesis, it enters the world of the senses, incarnating itself in the judge and becoming a concrete expression of will made manifest by his word.

The judge is the personification of law. Only from him can I expect in concrete instances that protection which I am promised in the abstract by the law. Only when the judge pronounces in my favor the word of justice do I learn that law is more than a vain shadow. For this reason we see that the true *fundamentum regnorum* rests in *iustitia* as well as in *ius*, for if the judge is not deft, the voice of the law remains as distant and as evanescent as the unattainable voice of dreams.

I cannot meet abstract law on the path I take as a man among men in society, for it only lives in the sidereal regions of the fourth dimension, but many times do I find you, O Judge, the corporeal evidence of the law, on whom depends the fate of my worldly goods.

How can I help but love you when I know that that continuous assistance in my every act which the law promises me can only be realized through your work? When I meet you on the road and bow to you with reverence, there is a sweetness of fraternal gratitude in my greeting. I know you are the keeper and the guardian of those things I hold most dear; in you I greet the peace of my hearth, my honor, and my liberty.

❖

In the last days of his life my father, also a lawyer, spoke these reassuring words: "The decisions of the courts are always just. In fifty-two years of practice I have never had occasion to complain of lack of justice. When I have won a case it was because my client was in the right; when I lost, the opposing party was in the right."

Is this a naïve statement? Perhaps. But only by this holy naïveté can the bar raise itself from a low game of intrigue and deceit to a noble instrument for the furtherance of social peace.

CHAPTER II

On Etiquette (or Discretion) in the Court

As long as the judicial process was thought of as a duel between the parties, with the judge acting merely as a referee, keeping the score and enforcing the rules of the game, it was only natural that the lawyer's most effective weapon was showmanship, and that his value was judged by sporting criteria, as it were. With a bon mot which in no way aided in clarifying the issue, but which put the opposing party at a disadvantage, the lawyer won the plaudits of the public, much as the star football player does by a spectacular play. In those days, when the lawyer rose to speak, he used to turn toward the audience with gestures reminiscent of the pugilist entering the ring ostentatiously flexing his biceps.

But in these times when everyone knows that even a civil case is not a game but rather the fulfillment by the state of its highest and most jealously guarded function, the courtroom is no longer the scene of sporting encounters. Lawyers are no longer circus performers nor salon lecturers; justice has become a serious thing.

❖

"SOMETIMES I wonder," a judge once confided to me, "whether the extraordinary conduct of some lawyers in court is not an indication of their poor breeding."

When these men are not in court they behave in a courteous and proper manner; they know what is done and what is not done and they act accordingly. If you meet one of them on the street and stop to chat a moment, his company is a pleasure; he knows that a gentleman does not raise his voice in conversation; he refrains from using high-sounding language to express simple things; he is careful not to interrupt any other speaker, and he avoids tormenting his listeners with long-winded rhetorical phrases. When he enters a shop to buy a necktie he does not find it necessary to emphasize the colors he wants by pummeling the counter with his fists, nor does he feel impelled to grimace at tea or to point his fingers at his hostess. But when he appears in court this cultured person forgets all he knows of good manners. With ruffled hair and contorted face he ejects a series of unnatural guttural sounds, adopting strange gestures and a new vocabulary, and sometimes, I have observed, even changing the pronunciation of certain consonants. It is as if he fell into a trance and through his inert body were speaking the spirit of some charlatan, who had escaped from the depths of hell.

Surely this must be the answer, for how else can the actions of such a man be logically explained—a man who, in an effort to impress the court with the merits of his case, considers it expedient so to shout, gesticulate, and grimace that if he behaved in such a way at home before his innocent little children, he would be greeted with a clamorous storm of hilarity?

❖

It would be useful if among the various tests which candidates for the bar were forced to undergo, a test of nervous resistance were included, like the one required of aspiring aviators. A good lawyer does not lose his head when some statement he has made is turned against him; he does not respond to the ruses of his adversary with the traditional old school gesture of grabbing his inkwell as if to hurl it at his enemy. The lawyer's must always be an understanding and reasoning passion; his nerves must be so disciplined that he can respond to insult with a friendly smile and can bow graciously to the judge who tells him to be silent. Vociferation is not an indication of energy, nor is sudden violence a sign of true courage. If a lawyer loses his head during a trial, it is reasonably certain that his client will lose the case.

❖

THE lawyer who believes that he can intimidate a judge by his screaming brings to mind that peasant who, when he lost something, instead of reciting prayers to Saint Anthony, the finder of lost things, began to abuse him with a string of oaths, justifying his impious action with these words: "If you want results, don't pray to saints, frighten them."

❖

THE aphorism, *Iura novit curia*, is not merely a rule of legal procedure that expresses the judge's duty to find the legal norm fitting the case without waiting for the parties to present it to him; it is also a rule of forensic etiquette, showing that if a lawyer would win his case, he would do well not to appear to teach the judges those things which good manners compel him to assume they already know. The man who adopts classroom tactics in court, ostentatiously showing off his knowledge, burdening the court with unusual and erudite concepts, may well be a great jurist, but he is a poor psychologist and, therefore, an inferior lawyer.

I am reminded of that old professor of legal medicine who, discovering that one of his pupils in preparing for the examination was attempting to master a difficult modern treatise instead of studying the professor's own outmoded text, said to him with a suspicious air, "Young

man, it looks as if you were trying to learn more than
I know about the subject," and then flunked him.

✧

"I have confidence in lawyers," a judge once said to me,
"because they openly admit they are defending one of the
parties and confess their bias; but I am wary of certain
professors of law who, without signing the briefs or appearing openly 'of counsel,' send in with the documents
of the case (almost as if we were their pupils) certain
opinions called *Per la Verità*[1] almost as if they would
have us believe that they were not being partisan in
these professional consultations, but that they were
disinterested scholars quite above worldly cares. For two
reasons I think this practice is in poor taste: first because, although the *consilium sapientis* served a useful
purpose in the days when the judges were illiterate, the
condescending attitude behind these little lessons is
hardly complimentary to a present-day judge, well
versed in legal knowledge; second, because it is difficult to
understand why, in these opinions inserted along with
the party's briefs, the Truth, with a capital T, always
coincides with the interest of the party seeking the
opinion."

"At least one *jurisconsult* agreed with me," added the
judge, "who himself had been a very erudite scholar, as
he recited to me a passage from Scaccia[2] which went like
this: *Ego cuidam, contra cuius causam allegabatur consilium antiqui et valentis doctoris, dicebam: amice, si
pars adversa, quae eo tempore litigabat, adivisset prius*

---

[1] "In the interest of Truth."
[2] Sigismondo Scaccia, Genevese jurist of the early XVII century.
His most noted work is *Tractatus de commercis et cambio*, Roma,
1617.

illum dictorem cum pecunia, tu nunc in causa tua haveris
consilium illius pro te."[3]

❖

THE lawyer who is rash enough to criticize the judge
while pleading a case acts as unwisely as does the scholar
who criticizes the professor during an oral examination.

❖

IF the lawyer feels that the judge is not favorably inclined toward the legal principles for which he is con-
tending, he cannot argue with the judge as he could with
an equal. He must cajole him and prepare him to be told
that he is wrong by first assuring him that they are
really in perfect agreement.

From this uncomfortable situation arises the frequent
use in forensic parlance of the device of "preterition"—
the rhetorical hypocrisy which flourishes with the use of
such well-worn phrases of the courtroom as the lawyer's
avowal when he wants to remind the judge of some legal
doctrine that he is merely "reminding himself of it."

A typical example of this expedient occurred when a
lawyer was pleading a point before a court which had
already decided the question one way and later reversed
itself in a subsequent decision. On this third occasion
the lawyer prefaced his remarks in this wise: "The question which I bring before you can be decided in only two
ways. This most excellent Court has already decided it
twice; the first time one way, the second time the other."
He paused and then, with a bow, continued, "And in
each case, most admirably."

[3] I said to a man whose adversary was represented by a learned
and venerable scholar, "My friend, if the other party to the suit had
been the first to offer that man money, you would now have his
counsel on your side."

I love the toga, not for the gold braid that adorns it nor for the voluminous sleeves which lend solemnity to one's gestures, but for its stylized uniformity, for its impersonality which covers the individual differences and the inequalities of men with the symbol of a function. The toga, equal for all, transforms him who wears it into a lawyer, a defender of rights, just as he who sits on the bench is a judge, nameless and untitled.

It is bad taste for a lawyer to let protrude from his toga the personality of Professor Tizio or Commendatore Caio,[4] just as it would be out of place to address the judge as "Giuseppe" or the public prosecutor as "Gaetano." Even the wigs of the British barristers, which may seem at first a ridiculous anachronism, serve the purpose of bringing the function to the fore and minimizing the man. The man may be bald or gray but before the court the lawyer is ageless and changeless.

❖

IF a judge forgets a lawyer's face and his name, his voice and his gestures, and still remembers the arguments which, coming forth from that nameless toga, won the case—that man is a great lawyer.

❖

JUSTICE has no use for those lawyers who go to court with the sole purpose of displaying their vaunted oratorical prowess. The lawyer should direct his energies to the task of clarifying the facts and the issues of the case, keeping his own personality well in the background; he should seem to emulate these modern indirect-lighting systems in which the source of the light remains hidden and the objects illuminated seem to glow with an internal radiance of their own, and not produce the bla-

4 Tizio and Caio are the Italian John Doe and Richard Roe.

tant effect of the old-fashioned light bulbs whose dazzling brightness obscures the objects they are intended to illumine.

❖

IF a lawyer insists upon speaking of himself in court rather than of the case at hand, he is as guilty of bad taste as if he should take off his toga in the middle of his address in order to show the court that he is patronizing the best tailor in town.

❖

A lawyer should be able to suggest the arguments which will win his case so subtly to the judge that the latter believes he has thought of them himself.

❖

THERE can be no justice without meticulous honesty; and this means, among other things, that there can be no justice without punctuality, a special kind of honesty to be practiced in the daily routine of administration.

Let this apply to the lawyer, whose honesty is continually shown in the care with which he arranges the documents of the case, in the neatness of his toga, in the clarity of his writing, in the brevity of his speech, in the diligence with which he remembers to file his briefs on the appointed day.

Let this apply to the judge, as well, whose honesty does not only consist in his incorruptibility but also, for example, in his care never to make the lawyers and the parties waste hours in the halls awaiting the opening of a hearing.

CHAPTER III

On Certain Similarities and Differences
Between Judge and Lawyer

Advocati nascuntur iudices fiunt.[1] This is not true in
the sense that one can be a good lawyer without training; it means that the qualities of combativeness and
impetuosity prized in a lawyer belong to passionate and
excessive youth, while only the passing of time matures
the qualities of wisdom and reflection which are the essential attributes of a good judge. A judge is a lawyer
mellowed and purified by age, a man from whom the
years have taken the illusions, exaggerations, prejudices, and perhaps even the impulsive generosity of
youth. The judge is what remains after there have been
removed from the lawyer all those exterior virtues which
the crowd admires.

The lawyer is the eager, generous youth of the judge;
the judge is the mellowed, ascetic old age of the lawyer.
The British system in which the high judges are chosen
from among the older lawyers is a practical confirmation
of this psychological development.

✧

THE aphorism, *Nemo iudex sine actore,*[2] is not only a
principle of jurisprudence; it has a much wider psychological implication as well. It shows that it is not shame-
ful laziness but an institutional necessity of his function
which makes the judge maintain a passive attitude during the judicial process, waiting without impatience or

1 Lawyers are born, judges are made.
2 No judge without a plaintiff.

curiosity for others to come before him with problems to resolve.

The judge's inertia is the guarantee of his equilibrium and impartiality. Action for him would always be partisan. The lawyer, who need not fear appearing partial, is the propelling organ of the judicial process; he must take the initiative, question the weak points, cut through the delays—in short, act, not only in the procedural sense of the word, but in the material sense as well.

The judge is static, the lawyer dynamic. This difference of function is apparent even in the external characteristic of the trial; the judge is seated, the lawyer stands; the judge holds his head in his hands, collected and immobile; the lawyer waves his tentacular arms, aggressive and unrequited. The contrast between the two types is apparent even in their vices, which are only the distorted images of their virtues. The lawyer in a fury of activity may make such a disturbance that he is asked to leave the courtroom; the judge by an excess of concentration may simply fall asleep.

❖

It may be that the lawyer's function requires more genius and imagination than the judge's. There is certainly a more difficult technical problem involved in finding good arguments than in selecting the better of those presented to you. But what a moral responsibility lies in that choice! When a lawyer has accepted a case his road is clear; he is like the soldier before a target. But the judge needs a force of character which the lawyer may lack; he must have the courage to exercise the almost divine function of rendering judgment, while constantly feeling within him the weakness and perhaps even the meanness of man. He must know how to silence an unrequited voice which asks what he would have done in his weakness had he been placed in the position of the litigant. He must be so sure of his duty that each time he decides a case he can forget that eternal admonition which comes to him from the Mountain: "Judge not."

❖

I love the judge because I feel that I am made of the same flesh and blood. I respect him because I feel he is twice as worthy as I, a mere lawyer. If the technique of embryology could be extended to the field of psychology, it would be found that the soul of a judge is composed of two lawyers in embryo, facing each other, like the Biblical twins who were struggling against each other even in the womb. The highest virtue of the judge, impartiality, is the result of this psychological conflict. The lawyer should not fret if the judge does not appear attentive to his arguments, for in order to reach a decision the judge must listen carefully to the two debaters who argue long and passionately within the cloister of his conscience.

❖

A Spanish lawyer, taking part in a criminal case in our country, was surprised to find that the lawyer's place in the courtroom was not raised to the level of the judge's bench, as it would be in Spain; he considered the Spanish custom a symbol of the equality of the two professions.

Someone suggested that the difference of position might depend upon the conception of the lawyer's function, that the equal level would correspond to a liberal and individualistic conception, while the lower position, symbolizing the subjection of the lawyer to the judge, would express the justice of an authoritarian regime.

I hold that the contrary is true. In a liberal conception of justice, the lawyer represents individual interests and so is naturally considered inferior to the judge, who represents the state. In an authoritarian regime the lawyer becomes more and more an instrument of public interests and is, like the judge, a servant of the state, sharing with the judge the dignity of being an essential organ of justice.

In a system such as ours, where the lawyer is invested with public functions, he is placed morally if not materially on the same plane with the magistrate. The judge who does not respect the lawyer or the lawyer who does not respect the judge forgets that the two professions are like communicating vases. The level of one cannot be lowered without equally affecting the level of the other.

❖

THE lawyer's defects react adversely on the judge and vice versa. The obscure, prolix and quibbling lawyer induces inattention and mental isolation on the part of the judge, who extends this new-born diffidence to the entire profession and forms the habit of ignoring all lawyers and treating them as necessary evils of the judicial process, which must be endured with a resignation passive even to the point of sleep. Through the fault of one bad lawyer, the judge refuses to avail himself of the valuable aid which good lawyers are eager to extend him.

In the same way a lazy inattentive judge leads lawyers to superficiality and bad legal practices. How many exceptions for incompetence and requests for unnecessary witnesses would the lawyers gladly pass over had not experience taught them that certain judges, having failed really to study the case, are disposed to accept with closed eyes every procedural objection and look with favor on all statements of witnesses so long as they do not cover more than four lines.

After all, judges are only human; they tend to follow the line of least resistance, and the clever lawyer is wont to strew his defense with bypaths which induce the judge to neglect the main road and wander into Elysian fields of mental inertia.

Instead of being a malicious manoeuvre by which the lawyer complicates the judge's task, procedural objections are often offered in respectful homage to the judge's health with the hope of making his task easier.

✧

I fear the judge who is too sure of himself, who reaches his decision quickly, jumping immediately to conclusions without deliberation or repentance. To use a military metaphor, the lawyer should resemble the *bersagliere* in his alertness and fighting spirit while the judge should emulate the *alpino* in his careful and stolid reasoning.[8]

✧

ONCE I saw a country lad pull off the long antennae of one of those black beetles which entomologists call *cerambici longicorni*; then he placed it on the edge of the road to watch with the wanton cruelty of children how the mutilated insect struggled to get out of his difficulty. Deprived of his exploratory organs, the poor insect staggered on his fragile legs, now swaying from side to side, now turning in circles. Every so often he ran into a blade of grass and even this was enough to turn him over on his back. This picture is recalled to me whenever I

8 The *bersaglieri* are the troops with the black chicken feathers on their hats. They march in double time and frequently ride motorcycles. The *alpini* are skiing alpine troops who guard the passes from Germany. They are principally composed of Northern Italians and are perhaps the most respected unit in the Italian army.

think what the judicial process would become if, as some people suggest, the lawyers, those sensitive antennae of justice, were eliminated.

❖

A judge does not need superior intelligence. It is enough that he be possessed of an average intellect so that he can understand *quod omnes intellegunt*. He must, however, be a man of superior moral attainments in order to be able to forgive the lawyer for being more intelligent than he.

❖

THE lawyer who complains that the judge has misunderstood him, discredits only himself. It is not the judge's duty to understand, but it is the lawyer's duty to make himself understood. The judge remains seated awaiting a communication; the lawyer is on his feet; he should be the aggressor and approach the judge in both the physical and the intellectual sense.

❖

AMONG all judicial offices, it seems to me the most arduous is that of the prosecuting attorney. As prosecutor he must be as partisan as a lawyer, and as guardian of the law he must be as impartial as the judge.

A lawyer without passion, a judge without impartiality—these are the psychological paradoxes which the prosecuting attorney must resolve. If he does not possess an exquisite sense of equilibrium he is in constant danger either of being so charmed by the serene detachment of the spectator as to lose the fighting spirit of the combatant, or of becoming so engrossed in the lawyer's problems as to forget the judge's impassible objectivity.

CHAPTER IV

On Forensic Oratory

WHEN two or more cultured and reasonable people want
to come to some agreement on a technical question, or to
persuade a third party to follow their advice—such as
businessmen signing a contract or doctors called in con-
sultation, generals collaborating on an offensive—in
each case their methods would be the same: an inter-
change of brief phrases would ensue in which each would
present his essential idea in simple words, the objections
would be heard and refuted singly until the point of basic
disagreement was reached. Sentences would be broken off
in the middle when the speaker realized that his meaning
was already clear, and gestures, facial expressions and
tones of voice would establish intercommunication and
understanding more expeditiously than the best turned
phrases.

This is the method sensible men have always used to
convince each other and to reach a mutually satisfac-
tory understanding. But lawyers, those professional per-
suaders, frequently employ an entirely different method.
Here tiresome monologue replaces rapid dialogue, the
stimulant of objection and interpolation is abolished or
deferred. Here one is considered a good speaker if he can
complete a complicated and exquisitely balanced sentence in one breath, even if after the first words it was
clear to all how it would end. Here it is permitted to
dwell at length over points on which all are agreed, to
cover aridness with useless or even fallacious rhetorical
ornamentation. Interruptions are not tolerated, each
person delivers his own aria, fixing his own mental scheme

much like the juggler who never turns his gaze from the chair he is precariously balancing on the end of his nose.

This method of procedure, which is the antithesis of that which reasonable people use, is sometimes referred to as forensic oratory.

✧

In order to extirpate any *bel canto* tendencies from pleadings before the bar, tendencies which have discredited all forms of oral argument in the eyes of the judges, it would be well to use a small courtroom and to seat the lawyers and the judges sufficiently close together to see each other's eyes while speaking, and to discern the degree of pleasure or pain evoked by their rhetorical conceits. A large courtroom which forbids any degree of intimacy leads the lawyer to force his tones, just as a warm bath induces him to sing. How can one help raising his voice and exaggerating his gestures in the vast hall of the United Sessions of the Supreme Court, a hall so large that the lawyer feels lost and insignificant among all the columns, and vaguely discerns the judges in the distance behind the high bench, looking like idols on an altar seen through a telescope in reverse? That hall, with its ornate solemnity, cries for "oratory." True, as a corrective medicine the architect has written around the walls a four-word maxim, with one word for each wall: *Veritas nimium altercando amittitur*.[1] On the wall facing the speaker, far off, above the heads of the august justices stands forth the *nimium*, as golden as silence, and when amid a wave of eloquence he glances at it, grasping its meaning, he concludes as quickly as he can.

[1] Truth is lost through too much disputation.

I would counsel the eager young lawyer who dreams of the day he shall be a famous attorney lavishing his eloquence on the Supreme Court, to visit Rome and attend a session of the Civil section of the court. Thus he will see how greatly his dreams differ from the reality. (And the contrast would be even more pronounced if he should look in the next room, where a Criminal section was meeting.)

If he had the patience to observe an entire sitting of say three to four hours, he would hear about eight cases, each taking less than a half-hour. In each case, after a brief summary of the facts by the *relatore*, he would hear an address by plaintiff's counsel, then one by defendant's counsel, and finally one by the state's attorney. Each of these addresses take from eight to ten minutes, hardly enough time, according to the classical rules, for getting through the preliminary phases of an oration; and if a lawyer should speak for more than ten minutes, the court would censure him for his prolixity. The young lawyer would leave the hall in a melancholic mood, but he would also be filled with admiration for two forms of heroism, that of the attorneys who succeeded in presenting all they had to say in a clear and sober manner within the space of ten minutes, without stammering from haste or without anxiety for the fleeting time, and that of the judges who every afternoon year in, year out, impassibly withstand the awful fate of hearing twenty-four addresses in a period of three hours.

❖

THE classical definition of a lawyer, *Vir bonus dicendi peritus*,[2] does not quite satisfy either the judge or the

[2] An honest man skilled in speech.

lawyer. Each would touch up the definition a little in his own way.

The lawyer would say: "Probity is certainly the essential virtue of the lawyer in the sense that he must never affirm anything he knows is untrue. But since the lawyer is obliged to secrecy, since he must never betray his client, he should know when and how to be silent and how to find in that silence a conciliation of his loyalty to the judge and his duty to his client."

The judge would say: "An honest lawyer is certainly a valued ally in the cause of justice, but since I must suspect him of trying to deceive me in the interest of his client when he speaks, his probity manifests itself rather in his silence than in his speech. The pleasantest token of loyalty which a lawyer can offer a judge, one which spares him suspicion, doubts, and delay, is silence, for it is in the knowledge of keeping silent that a lawyer most advantageously displays his learning and his discretion." And so by following different arguments the judge and the lawyer come finally to the same conclusion and concur in correcting the definition to read *Vir bonus tacendi peritus*, an honest man skilled in silence.

❖

I do not believe that we need to teach our law students the art of forensic oratory as was done in the classical schools of rhetoric. The law schools should bend every effort toward developing the art of clear thinking. This once acquired, the art of clear speaking will come of itself.

But if courses in forensic oratory were to be included I would want them organized in this way: the student would be given a single morning to study a complicated Civil case, on which he would be asked to report orally

in a clear and complete manner for the inexorable period
of an hour. The following day he would be asked to present the same material in a half an hour, and on the third
day he would present the entire case clearly and concisely in a quarter of an hour.

This third report would be given before a group of
students who knew nothing of the case. If the speaker
could succeed in presenting the case so well that the students could grasp the essential points, he would show he
had mastered that type of oratory which makes a great
lawyer.

❖

A really useful defense is never a drawn-out monologue;
it is a living dialogue between the lawyer and the judge,
who should respond with his eyes, with gestures, with
questions.

The lawyer should be pleased with these interruptions
as they show that the judge is not unmoved by or ex-
traneous to the discussion. Interruption means reaction
and reaction is the best acknowledgment of a stimulus.

The judicial process will have approached perfection
when the discussion between judge and lawyer is as free
and natural as that between persons, mutually respect-
ing each other, who try to explain their points of view
for their common good.

Such an arrangement would be a loss for forensic oratory but a gain for justice.

❖

THE lawyer's harangue is frequently taken by the judge
as a period of mental relaxation. He returns to the
courtroom in spirit when the lawyer has finished.

❖

IF a man who knew nothing of legal procedure should

enter a court during a trial he would naturally wonder to whom the lawyer's eloquence was addressed, and he would never suspect that the audience was really that little group of bored and distraught old men with their heads in their hands seated high up at the back of the room on the judges' bench. The uninitiated person who was observing the scene for the first time would suppose that the orator with his ridiculous gesticulations was merely talking for the joy of hearing the reverberations of his own voice, as other people enjoy singing or doing setting-up exercises, and that the other people in the courtroom were not there to listen but were patiently waiting for him to finish so they could get about their own work.

The lawyer's defense, instead of being an integrating part of the process, has become a parenthesis, an intermission placed in the middle of the trial, just as in the old plays they used to insert a ballet during which the actors rested and the audience could slumber peacefully without fear of losing the thread of the plot.

❖

A judge's opinion on forensic oratory: Clarity and brevity are the most admirable qualities of oratory; they are most eloquently expressed in silence.

❖

By a reaction which is almost acoustical the lawyer senses when his words are convincing the judge and when they are leaving him doubtful or suspicious. It seems a phenomenon of resonance. Sometimes the arguments which come from the mouth of the lawyer are in harmony with the disposition of the judge and they make him vibrate. Sometimes the lawyer's voice sounds false and without echo, as if isolated in a void. And then, the more he forces his tones to overcome this handicap, the more difficult it becomes to get in tune with his audience.

✧

"REMEMBER that clarity and brevity are the two qualities that the judge likes best in a lawyer."

"And when I can not be both brief and clear at the same time, which quality should be sacrificed in order to least displease the judge?"

"When a judge is put to sleep by prolixity, even clarity is useless. Brevity is better though the meaning be obscured. When a lawyer speaks little, the judge may not be certain of the lawyer's meaning; nevertheless he is certain he is right."

✧

I am not moved by the tears of those who bewail that with the advent of our new Criminal procedure, limiting as it does the length of the plea for the defense, fine oratory is to be excluded from the courtroom.

In the first place I am loath to appraise the value of a lawyer's defense purely on esthetic grounds. When I hear such adjectives as beautiful and brilliant applied to a lawyer's address, I feel they are out of place. These are attributes befitting lecturers, but to apply them to the sober austere profession of the bar seems frivolous and almost irreverent.

But even considering forensic oratory as an art, it is well known there has never been a spectacle more esthetically humiliating than the performance of the old-fashioned criminal lawyer who ranted through three or four straight sittings of the court seemingly unable to unwind himself, giving the painful impression of being inextricably caught on the windmill of his own eloquence. Art is measure and discipline. And if there be anyone who still seeks artistic achievement through the medium of the lawyer's plea, he should applaud the legislators who in limiting the length of the plea have brought the field of oratory back from the anarchy of free verse to the salutary restraint of art.

✧

THAT day I was at my best. I was aware of the affectionate sympathy of the judges when I sat down. They smiled upon me with such warmth that it almost seemed that through a miracle of love their arms, wrapped in their black cloaks, were suddenly lengthened by several yards so they could reach down and caress me.

This all happened, if I remember correctly, the day I arose to say: "The defense rests."

✧

LIKE architecture, forensic oratory tends to become rational—direct lines, unadorned walls, no useless ornamentation, frank ostentation instead of dissimulation of functionally necessary elements. The orator as well as the architect should primarily consider the solidarity of his construction—all the better if from this structural solidarity an unsought monumental beauty should burst forth.

But this abolition of ornamental figures of speech would be an undertaking not without danger. I fear that if the embellishments were torn from certain orations, as from certain façades, instead of finding a solid foundation beneath, there would be only fragile stucco.

✧

IN certain sections of Italy a practice has arisen for handling Civil cases which is perhaps illegal, but which seems to me to have all the advantages of an oral hearing without the inconvenience of orations. Instead of the solemn hearing before the entire bench, which is inattentive and ill-informed, the discussion takes place in the judges' chambers after the *relatore* has had time to study the case and to present the facts to his brother judges. This system has two advantages: in the first place, the lawyer is talking to persons who know the facts of the case and are therefore competent to evaluate his arguments; and in the second place, he is forced to present his case in an informal manner as if at a round-table without the pomp and circumstance of the courtroom.

Before speech, which means the simple concise expressions of thought, reassumes its just position, oratory, which means the rhetorical device of hiding one's thought beneath an avalanche of words, must be removed from the courtroom. Gestures and poses must be abolished; distances must be reduced. Oratory is in good part a question of mimicry: force an orator to sit down and he'll soon change his tune. Somehow I can't picture Cicero complacently sitting at a table as he was inveighing against Cataline.

❖

WHY is it that when a judge meets a lawyer in a tram or in a café and converses with him, even if they discuss a pending case, the judge is more disposed to believe what the lawyer says than if he said the same thing in court during the trial? Why is there greater confidence and spiritual unity between man and man than between judge and lawyer?

The great lawyer is the man who succeeds in speaking to the judge in court as simply and as concisely as he would speak to him in a café. He is the man who can convince the judge he is as trustworthy at the bar of justice as at the bar of the café.

✧

A judge once remarked of a defense whose rhetorical embellishments had left him so esthetically satisfied by the form that he was suspicious of the content: "It reminds me of the rose which was so perfect it seemed artificial."

✧

THE most malicious thing a judge can do to a lawyer is to let him talk on without interrupting him when he is talking uselessly or to the detriment of his client.

✧

To the trained ear of the judge the lawyer's tone of voice is sometimes more important than the words he speaks. When a lawyer forces his voice in some phase of his address in an effort not to appear false, a peculiar sound results, perhaps like what a doctor must hear through his stethoscope when he has located the disease.

✧

WHEN a client attends the hearing of his case he is not pleased unless his lawyer speaks last, because it is a common belief that in a debate he who speaks last usually wins.

But the client does not realize that even among judges one finds diffident and contrary natures from whom an argument provokes an irrepressible need for refutation. When one encounters such a judge it is better that the last advocate to stimulate this reaction be your adversary.

In this case the proverb is reversed. He who speaks last is always wrong.

A JUDGE spoke thus at the end of a hearing: "Who said that oral discussion was useless in Civil cases? Before the lawyer's harangues I was in doubt. After plaintiff's counsel had spoken, I knew I should decide in favor of defendant, but then, fortunately for the plaintiff, defendant's counsel spoke and I was convinced justice was with the plaintiff after all."

The client does not realize that instead of congratulating his own lawyer on winning the case in some instances he should be grateful to his adversary's counsel.

❖

CONSIDERING the way certain lawyers speak and write I sometimes wonder whether the function of counsel is not to show the weaknesses rather than the strength of his client's case. In these instances the clever judge can find the case of one party in the defense of the other.

CHAPTER V

On a Certain Immobility of Judges on the Bench

It must be a painful necessity which requires the judge to listen to the fatuous arguments of some lawyers. In order to prevent this annoyance the judge may have recourse to one of two alternatives: either the speaker must be silenced, and the energetic judge brings this about by interrupting him; or the listener must stop listening, and the passive judge brings this about by falling asleep.

❖

I believe that many times judges' sleep is premeditated. It is a voluntary procedure which relieves them of the burden of hearing what a lawyer has to say and still permits them to decide the case in favor of his client on their own grounds.

Many times sleep is the expedient by which the judge protects one of the parties from the errors of his lawyer.

❖

I like the judge who looks me in the eyes while I am speaking. He does me the honor of going behind my words, which after all may only be a clever façade, to search for an honest conviction in my soul.

I like the judge who interrupts me while I am speaking. I seek to help him, and when he asks me to stop as if to warn me that a continuation of my address might bore him, he acknowledges that up to that moment he has not been bored.

To perhaps a lesser degree I like the judge who sleeps while I am speaking. Sleep is the most discreet method which the judge has at his command for quietly tiptoeing away when what I have to say no longer interests him, thus leaving me to talk to myself in peace.

❖

A JUDGE once told me of his professional experience with sleep brought on by tiresome attorneys.

"It is not true that sleep is insidious; it faithfully gives warning of its approach. A man who is listening to a speech knows he is about to fall asleep when the meaning of the words begins to disappear and the sound of the voice, though still distinct, takes on a diffuse and mysterious resonance like the rhythmical incantation of the snake-charmer's flute. This acoustical purification of the words which transforms them, or better, dissolves them into music is, to the wise, a forewarning of the magical state about to overcome him.

"Careless lawyers do not realize that in modulating their voices and in giving to their sentences a cadenced sonority they facilitate and hasten that fatal disassociation of meaning from sound. It is enough that one of those practitioners of vocal esthetics utters his first phrases; immediately the judge loses the train of thought, abandoning himself to the magic of the sound. And the rest comes of itself."

❖

"THERE exist sounds *in rerum natura* which at certain times in certain places seem by their rhythmical repetition the embodiment of somnolence; as, for instance, the strumming of grasshoppers on a summer evening, the distant croaking of frogs in the sultry stillness preceding a thunderstorm, even the buzzing of flies in the squalid room of a third-class hotel."

A Civil judge, as he was getting a breath of air in the corridor during a court recess, called this to my attention. It was a stifling July afternoon. The court usher, seated on a bench, was wiping the perspiration from his face with his dirty gown, and through the closed doors of the Criminal courtroom came, from time to time the emphatic exasperation of a defending attorney's voice, like a nasal gargle in an unknown language, poorly transmitted over the radio.

❖

Observe how many concert-goers keep their eyes open during a concert and you will better understand the meaning of the compliment a judge pays a lawyer when, at the end of a hearing, he says: "Your address was like a musical composition."

❖

A judge with a certain sense of humor was once speaking to a professor of legal procedure.

"You spend your life," he said, "teaching students what the judicial process is; if you would impress upon them what the judicial process is not, you would turn out better lawyers. For instance, it is not a stage where actors display their talents; neither is it a show-window where merchandise is advertized; it is not a hall for lecturers, nor a salon where dilettantes exchange bon mots; it is neither a chess club, nor a fencing ground."

"Nor a dormitory," timidly added the professor.

CHAPTER VI

On the Relationship Between the Lawyer and the Truth,
or on the Necessary Partisanship of the Lawyer

LIKE the antagonism between the devil and holy water, the conflict between the lawyer and the truth is an ancient one. Among the remarks on the professional prevarication of lawyers the following line of reasoning is typical: "In every lawsuit there are two lawyers. One calls an object white and the other calls it black. They cannot both be speaking the truth, since their statements of fact are contradictory. Therefore one of them is sustaining a falsehood." This reasoning leads to the conclusion that fifty per cent of the lawyers are liars. And, since the attorney who wins one case will lose another, it would seem that sooner or later every lawyer will take a case which can not be defended honestly, and this makes liars of them all.

This reasoning does not take into account the fact that truth has three dimensions and can appear differently to people observing it from different points of view.

In almost every instance both lawyers, although sustaining contradictory positions, do so in good faith because each presents the truth as it appears from the viewpoint of his client.

In a London gallery there is a famous painting by Champaigne showing Cardinal Richelieu in three different poses. In the center of the picture he is seen full face, and on each side he is shown in profile, facing the central figure. The model was the same in each case, yet there are three persons in the painting, each looking different.

It is the same with a lawsuit. The lawyers present the two profiles of truth, but only the judge in the center looks it full in the face.

❖

THE scales, the traditional symbol of justice, are the mechanical representation of the play of psychic forces which make the judicial process function. The competing lawyers must enter the picture, presenting their contrasting arguments so that the judge, after a few oscillations, may settle on the truth.

The further the opposing weights radiate from the center (or the point of impartiality) the more sensitive must be the mechanism, the more exact the measurement. As each lawyer presents the most favorable case possible for his client, between them they create the equilibrium which the judge is seeking. He who would blame the lawyers for their partiality should also blame the weights on the scales.

❖

A lawyer who tried to perform his function with impartiality would not only become a useless duplication of the judge, but would also be the latter's worst enemy: by failing to compensate for the partiality of his adversary, instead of aiding justice, he would encourage the victory of injustice.

A lawyer is like an artist in discovering and revealing the most secret and concealed aspects of truth. Laymen, lacking this talent, sometimes assume that the facts, lovingly and carefully assembled by a lawyer, are only an invention of his mind. But a lawyer does not alter the truth, he selects its most significant elements which may escape the perception of outsiders. It is unjust to accuse him of betraying truth in making this selection because, like the artist, he is its most sensitive interpreter.

✧

JUST as the magnanimity of the true historian gives to the heroic episode a significance which the chronicler fails to grasp, so in the judicial process (particularly in Criminal cases) the facts correspond to the intellectual and moral stature of the attorney. The public imagines that certain advocates choose to defend only those crimes which are motivated by a certain nobility of sentiment, a certain grandeur of passion. Perhaps it would be more accurate to say that these advocates have the faculty of discovering in even the most sordid crimes the elements of human goodness with which their own natures are most sympathetic and which would remain hidden from the general view, were it not for their generosity.

✧

PLACE two painters side by side before the same landscape, each with his own easel, and return an hour or so later to see what each has on his canvas. You will find two landscapes so different that it will seem impossible that they were drawn from the same model.

Would you say that one of the artists has betrayed the truth?

✧

WHEN you appraise the usefulness of the lawyer to the judicial process, do not look at one isolated individual whose unilateral activity taken by itself might seem to lead the judge astray, but consider the comple-

mentary function of the two adversaries—each justifying and necessitating the other's partiality.

The judge should be impartial; he is a unity, and he
is above the contestants; but the lawyers are meant to be
partial because truth is more easily understood if it is
approached from two directions. The partiality of one
lawyer reacts upon his adversary, inciting him to further efforts and, by the ensuing series of counterreac-
tions oscillating back and forth like a pendulum, the
judge is aided in determining the point of equilibrium—
justice.

❖

THE lawyers furnish the judge with the raw materials
from which he fashions a just solution—the chemical
synthesis of two opposing partialities. They should
always be thought of as a couple, even in the precise
mechanical use of the term: a system of two equal forces
operating in parallel lines in opposite directions, gen-
erating motion, giving life to the process, and finding
repose in justice.

❖

THE best proof of the purifying effect of a debate
between two lawyers, intended to absorb all polemical
intemperances in the air and to leave the judge in an
atmosphere of serenity, is found in the function of the
prosecuting attorney in Criminal cases whom the state
has set up as an official antagonist, thereby relieving the
judge of the necessity of reacting against the defending
attorney and unconsciously arriving at a state of mind
hostile to the defendant.

Thus in a Criminal action where the interest of the
parties could be represented by a single lawyer, the
state has felt impelled in the public interest to add a

second advocate to counterbalance the partiality of the defending attorney with an artificially created polemic above which the judge may preside with equanimity.

✧

EVERY lawyer's defense gives a chiaroscuro effect. Facts that are favorable to his client are well illuminated and others that weaken his case are left in darkness. But one lawyer's case is the complement of his adversary's and it is the judge's function to fit one over the other and thus fill out the picture. By this simple expedient he is able to reconstruct piece by piece the checkerboard of truth.

✧

THE lawyer treats reality as does the historian who selects his facts in accordance with a pre-established criterion, passing over other facts which, in the light of this criterion, appear irrelevant. Either lawyer or historian would betray his profession if he altered the truth by inventing facts; neither betrays it so long as he limits himself to collecting and co-ordinating from crude unrefined reality those aspects which are pertinent to the defense of his position.

CHAPTER VII

On Certain Aberrations of Clients, for Which the Judges Should Excuse the Lawyer

It is truly surprising to see with what regularity clients look for qualities in the lawyer which are incompatible with those the judges admire. Judges prefer lawyers who are discreet and laconic; clients want them verbose and overbearing. Judges despise the caviling prevaricator; clients see in the fertile excogitation of legal practices, devious in method and dubious in ethics, the highest expression of the lawyer's genius. Judges prefer the lawyer who relies on the objective validity of his arguments rather than on the weight of his personal influence; clients prefer lawyers who are members of Parliament or professors.

But strangest of all is the fact that whenever a judge seeks the benefit of counsel in some suit to which he is a party, he falls into the same error as the layman and lays his case before a lawyer of that very class which as a judge he scorns.

❖

What constitutes a great lawyer? He is a man who helps the judge reach a just decision and helps his client present his case.

Such a lawyer speaks no more than is necessary; he writes clearly and to the point; he does not encumber the courtroom with his personality. He does not bore the judges with his prolixity nor raise their suspicions with his subtlety. For all practical purposes, then, he is the opposite of that type whom many laymen consider the great lawyer.

THE client says of the lawyer he has chosen: "A smooth talker, knows all the tricks. A first-rate lawyer."

The judge says, in deciding against the client: "A windy little shyster, the worst kind of lawyer."

❖

CERTAIN clients come to a lawyer, confide their troubles to him, and then go home light-hearted, feeling that they have rid themselves of all their problems. They go to bed and fall fast asleep like innocent children, in the belief that the lawyer has assumed the professional duty to lie awake and worry on their account.

One evening I met a client of mine at the theater. He had been in that day to tell me he was on the brink of bankruptcy. He showed surprise and annoyance at finding me in a place of diversion, and throughout the performance he shot disapproving glances in my direction, as if to let me know that with ruin facing him I should be home bemoaning his fate and that it was, to say the least, indelicate of me to go out seeking entertainment.

❖

WHEN you explain to certain clients that lawyers are not made to cheat justice, they look at you with amazement. "What are they for then," they seem to ask, "if not to take upon themselves our difficulties and to preserve immaculate our reputations as respectable folk?"

❖

AT the end of an idle day when no client had come to knock at his door, a lawyer left his office rubbing his hands together and smiling happily, and was heard to say: "A fine day, no one has asked me to advance court costs."

AND usually with cause judges complain that lawyers write too much.

But they would be mistaken in ascribing this to innate verbosity or even to a desire for large fees. Judges do not realize how much of this prolixity is due to pressure from their clients; they do not take into consideration the tact required to convince some clients that the quality of a defense is not commensurate with its volume.

I shall always remember the words of a charming lady on leaving my office after having told me ten times over the points she considered essential to her case. Stopping at the door, she turned to me with an entreating smile and said: "I leave myself in your hands; write a lot."

❖

SOME good men who like to "live well" believe that a doctor is not intended to teach the methods of sane living which preserve health, but rather that his function is to cure the evil effects of overindulgence by the use of heroic remedies, in this manner blessedly permitting them to continue their unrepented excesses. Likewise there are persons who hold the lawyer's function is not to keep his clients within the bounds of legality, but is to extricate them from the consequences of their misdeeds, so that unpunished they may tranquilly and securely continue to disregard the letter and spirit of the law.

❖

I know of a lawyer who after being convicted of fraud was disbarred. After he had been released from prison a horde of clients came to him who would never have thought of consulting him as long as they believed he was honest.

This is the mentality of the public on the question

of lawyers. If he were able to cheat on his own hook, they say, he might be able to deceive the judges for them as well.

✧

THE difference between the true lawyer and those men who consider the law merely a trade is that the latter seek to find ways to permit their clients to violate the moral standards of society without overstepping the letter of the law, while the former look for principles which will persuade their clients to keep within the limits of the spirit of the law in common moral standards.

✧

A lawyer of my acquaintance was given a painting by a friend. (The latter was one of those men who, living with his head in the clouds, still believes that clients are usually the victims of unscrupulous lawyers whereas every one knows that the reverse is true.) The painting showed a thoroughly plucked chicken and it bore the following title: "Portrait of a client who has just won a case."

The lawyer sought the help of another friend of his, a philologist, and hung the picture on the wall of his waiting-room, after having appended the following inscription: *Non ego sic plumas evellere quaero clienti, felix ni raperet perfidus ille meas.*

Sometime later a nobleman who had been the lawyer's client for many years and who owed him a round sum of money for expenses, apart from any fees, came to the lawyer's office. As the lawyer was accompanying him to the door he saw the painting, and since he was quite ignorant of Latin, although a nobleman, he asked the lawyer to translate the inscription.

"Most gladly, sir," said the lawyer. "The inscription

says that I have no desire to reduce my clients to the condition of this miserable chicken, that on the contrary I should be quite content [and here the lawyer sighed a great sigh] if my clients did not pluck me."

At this the nobleman patted the lawyer on the shoulder in a very lordly manner and said as he was crossing the threshold: "How lucky you are to have a profession sufficiently remunerative to enable you to dabble with literature."

❖

THERE are certain phrases that a lawyer must learn to bear in silence without showing irritation and even with a smile on his face, particularly if the speaker, as is usually the case, happens to be a charming young lady. A typical phrase of this kind would sound something like this: "I have come to you because I thought it would be better to be gouged by an experienced extortioner." Or like this: "Rather than give my savings to that assassin [referring generally to the husband] I'd rather have them eaten up by lawyers." Upon hearing these delicate allusions to extortioners and executioners and to the greed of lawyers (always in the plural as if like jackals they went around in packs), one's first impulse is forcefully to eject the "lady" or the "gentleman" downstairs and out the door. One needs restraint and resignation to consider these little gems of impertinence in the light in which they are intended, that is, as compliments. The type of client who would make such remarks would be amazed at the lawyer's natural reaction, for in the language of these clients they are merely intended to convey to the lawyer the fact that he is reputed to be a prince of the forum.

IT is a difficult task to defend an ingenuous client who is completely ignorant of the devious ways of the law. When you speak of certain formalities which were not observed, or of irregularities of form, and you tell him that all is lost because of the statute of limitations, and he looks at you agape with an expression combining terror and admiration, quite incapable of fathoming the meaning of these terms, you are put in the uncomfortable position of one who, unwilling to play the magician, must run the risk of appearing an impostor in the eyes of the uninitiated.

But it is still more difficult to defend the client who considers himself a consummate jurist. Such a man is usually either a retired clerk who passes his old age in the public libraries scanning legal periodicals, or a gentleman farmer who some thirty years previously had gone through law school as a sort of diversion before peacefully retiring to his estate. When these men find themselves parties to a lawsuit, they go right to the codes themselves and succeed in finding the very articles which they are sure will fit their case. When they finally turn the case over to you, they tell you just how to plead it and assume that you really have nothing to do but follow their directions.

And woe to you if you fail to carry out their instructions. If you should then lose the case you can hardly imagine the vile language with which they will regale you, and even if you win they will have difficulty concealing their annoyance. Such clients as these will soon forget that in the end you won the lawsuit, but their pride as amateur jurists will keep ever fresh in their minds that you insulted them by neglecting to employ their suggestions in your pleadings.

CHAPTER VIII

On Litigiousness

THERE is a time when the lawyer must look reality in the face with the impassible eye of the judge. This is when a client asks his opinion as to the advisability of bringing suit. The lawyer must examine the question impartially, weighing the case for the other party against the case for his client, and he must decide whether the partial attitude he will be asked to assume as a trial attorney will further the cause of justice. Thus in Civil cases the lawyer must act as the examining magistrate, the preliminary investigating organ of the dispute. The lawyer's social usefulness can be measured by the number of times he advises his client that he has no cause of action.

✧

THE most valuable work of a lawyer takes place before suit is brought, when he attempts to reconcile the parties by his wise counsel, doing his best to prevent the dispute from reaching that state of morbid paroxysm which necessitates recourse to the judicial clinic. If some are inclined to doubt the effectiveness of doctors and lawyers in curing disease, they should not forget the great social utility of their prophylactic activities.

The honest lawyer should be more than a clinician of the legal profession, he should be a hygienist as well. Considering their daily work of disinfecting litigious persons, relieving the courtrooms of their disputes, judges should realize that lawyers, after all, are their most faithful collaborators.

SOME sarcastic unscrupulous person may say that the lawyer should exclusively consider legal questions, and should leave moral problems to the client. I deem it the high office of the lawyer first to suggest to the client his moral duty, and second his legal rights, and to make him understand that the Civil code is not intended to be a convenient screen for unethical conduct.

In a treatise or a lecture it is easy for a jurist to consider legal questions as theorems which can be demonstrated in abstract formula, where men are represented by letters and interests by numbers. The practicing attorney, however, must take into consideration the living men behind the formulae. So long as the professors continue to tell their pupils that the law applies equally to all, it is up to the lawyers to explain to their clients that private law has been made for honest people, and that the others are taken care of by the Criminal law.

❖

ACCORDING to Racine, sixty is the best age for litigiousness, "*le bel age pour plaider*." But every lawyer knows the type of client for whom all ages are the same. Even in youth, when others think of love and glory, the essential purpose of his life is litigation. Such men are not driven to this state by malice or avarice but by an insatiable morbid curiosity as to the future, a curiosity which every wise man hides deep in his heart each morning when he feels it rising within him.

The litigious man craves a lawsuit because it affords him the excitement of anticipating the decision. Defeat does not discourage him; it merely intensifies his interest in the contest. If he continually adds claims and causes of action it is not so much that he expects them to be upheld as it is that they create a series of steps

which prolongs the delightful suspense of awaiting the
final decision. What he fears is the termination of the
case, even if he wins; for it means to him the revelation
of the mystery, the disappearance of the risk, the end of
speculation. What has life to offer when the last decision has been handed down? *"Mais vivre sans plaider,
est-ce contentement?"*

I know a venerable litigant, now more than ninety
years old, who after the age of sixty brought a suit over
a disputed inheritance. His adversaries, who were then
young, thought the best tactics were to wear the old man
out by dilatory methods in order to hasten his death,
which they expected in the near future. Thus began an
epic duel between Civil procedure and longevity. As the
years have passed generations of lawyers have defended
the parties, and one by one the judges who handed down
the early decisions have gone to their last rest. The old
gentleman, instead of aging, seems to take on new life
from every procedural objection which further post-
pones the final decision. Even today, with his patriarchal
beard flying over pocketsful of *carta bollata*,[1] he fights
on undaunted against his adversaries who feel they are
bringing on his death by their procrastination. Little do
they realize that only victory would kill him.

❖

BUT we should guard against damning as a quarrelsome
nuisance every man who asks the court for redress
against overbearing or dishonest neighbors. We must
also be cautious in our joy when statistics show that
litigiousness is diminishing. Sometimes litigiousness is a
sign of morbid anti-social instincts. At other times it is

---

[1] Official stamped paper, on which legal documents must be written.

the result of the holy desire to protect society against malefactors and is evidence of an abundant faith in the administration of justice.

To litigate may mean (as in the case of the miller of Sans Souci[2]) to have faith in the effectiveness of the State. It may also entail actually rendering a favor to the State, for the State finds its highest expression in protecting rights, and therefore should be grateful to the citizen who, in demanding justice, gives it the opportunity to defend justice, which after all is the basic *raison d'être* of the State. We should not forget the tactics of Solon, who, according to Aristotle, wrote his famous code in obscure language so that many lawsuits would result, in this way giving the State ample opportunity to exercise and increase its authority over the citizens through frequent adjudication.

The day that I shall see the courts close for lack of suits, I shall not know whether there is occasion for joy or sorrow. I should be happy if it signified the advent of a new order in which man is no longer disposed to harm his neighbor, and in which universal love reigns supreme, but I should be melancholy, indeed, if it indicated that man is no longer willing to rebel against the impositions of others, and that universal vileness has triumphed.

❖

IT is difficult to determine where ends the courage which forbids us to bow our heads before the overbearing action of others and where begins that base and petulant litigiousness which is foreign to any sense of social toler-

2 This refers to a German legend of a miller who threatened to take Frederick the Great to court to protect his rights to his land, which Frederick wanted to buy.

ance and human understanding. This problem daily tor-
ments the lawyer's conscience. He knows that he would
betray his high office if he encouraged useless lawsuits,
but he would betray it still more gravely if he suppressed
in the heart of a just man his heroic intention to champion the cause of justice at his own risk.

❖

A certain type of client, found most frequently among
the poor and uncultured classes, has such a blind and
absolute faith in the skill of lawyers and the infallibility
of judges that they fill us with fear and with tenderness.
When I hear a client say, after I have expressed my honest doubts on the outcome of a case, "But, sir, if you try
I know you can win the case," I want to open his eyes
to all the hazards with which the lawyer's road is strewn.
But then I realize that his faith in justice, his belief that
she is a powerful goddess to whom one does not call in
vain, is perhaps the greatest achievement of civilization,
and is certainly the binding force which best holds
human society together.

And I have not the courage to disillusion such a man.

❖

CERTAIN lawyers who would consider it bad taste to sue
in their own names for a few paltry dollars still feel it is
their duty to protect their clients with equal zeal, regardless of the sum involved in the suit. Such men do not
degrade the profession; they honor it.

This is because the economic aspect of the suit is not
of personal interest to the lawyer who handles his client's
case. That is the client's problem. With the lawyer it is
a question of professional integrity. The client has
placed the protection of his rights in the hands of the

lawyer, and the smaller the pecuniary value of the case, the greater the human value it represents, for the lawyer feels more keenly the trust of the poor man who makes him the confidant of his distress.

CHAPTER IX

On the Predilection of Judges and Lawyers
for Questions of Law or for Questions of Fact

EVEN in judicial life the most useful talents are sometimes the least appreciated. There is a tendency among judges and lawyers to dismiss questions of fact from their consideration and to refer to certain persons in uncomplimentary tones as "sticklers for facts," and at the same time to extol and emulate that type of jurist who in seeking for general principles overlooks specific factual details.

But the man who sticks to the facts, be he judge or lawyer, is a good man. He is modest, perhaps, but honest; he is more concerned with finding the just solution most adequately covering the facts at hand than in cutting a fine figure as a contributor to a law journal. Placing the good of his clients above his own, he undertakes a laborious examination of their files, a task which requires abnegation and yields no glory.

It is unfortunate that, as the court system is actually arranged, the care with which the judge listens to evidence and the diligence with which he examines the documents are not known outside the courtroom, while the lucid reasoning and the brilliant style of his opinions are always accessible to those who would assay his ability. For this reason the judge who has a predilection for general principles is often thinking more of his own promotion than of the promotion of justice.

❖

ONCE upon a time there was a doctor who was called to the bedside of a sick man; and instead of questioning him and giving him a thorough examination in order to diagnose his disease, he propounded certain philosophical hypotheses on the metaphysical origin of disease, which from his point of view made it superfluous to take the patient's pulse or temperature. The relatives of the sick man listened to the doctor, astonished at his great knowledge. Meanwhile the patient peacefully expired.

If we should describe this doctor in legal terminology we should call him a "specialist in questions of law."

❖

THERE is an old maxim, full of wisdom, which reads: *Ex facto oritur ius*, "Law springs from reality." This maxim imposes upon the conscientious judge or lawyer a careful, almost pedantically painstaking, examination of the facts under discussion. But certain lawyers read the maxim inversely. When they are excogitating some brilliant theory of jurisprudence in the development of which they can display their virtuosity, they adjust the facts conveniently to the exigencies of the theory. Thus for them *ex iure oritur factum*.

❖

ONLY the pure jurist, who writes treatises or teaches in a law school, can afford the luxury of having set opinions on certain legal questions and of openly opposing the prevailing doctrine when he thinks it is in error; the humble practicing attorney must be careful to maintain an elasticity of opinion on matters for judicial interpretation so that he will always be able and willing to follow the prevailing opinion whenever he is defending a client, for thus backed by the most accredited authorities he will be more certain of victory. He is a poor lawyer who knows not how to resist the temptation to test *in corpore vile* the practical validity of his own theories; for when

one is dealing with the living flesh of a client, even if the
jurist in him is certain that the prevailing theories are
quite erroneous, discretion should move the attorney in
him to hold to the maxim, *Video meliora proboque dete-
riora sequor.*[1]

✧

"ELEGANT questions of law"—these are useless paren-
theses of subtlety and bravura, which serve only to dis-
tort the simple human qualities which underlie the case;
they are similar to those acrobatic variations which
certain virtuosos of the violin delight in inserting in the
middle of the simplest, most direct, and most inspired
sonatas.

✧

IT is frequently said that oral testimony is the typical
instrument of procedural bad faith and that justice can
expect nothing but betrayal from witnesses, who are
forgetful when they are not corrupt. This may be true,
but I wonder whether the traditional complaint against
parole evidence has not been brought about for the most
part by the ineptitude or laziness of those who receive it.

In some courts the judges responsible for the taking
of preliminary evidence (perhaps because they are over-
burdened with other responsibilities) turn over this
delicate task to minor court officials, and this leads one
to think that if the witnesses do not always tell the truth,
the fault is not altogether theirs. A wise judge, with a
deep understanding of human nature, who can afford to
take the time and who does not feel that he is demeaning
himself in so doing, can always squeeze out from even the
most obtuse and reluctant witness some precious drop
of truth.

[1] I see the better way and I approve, though I follow the lesser.

In the professional training of magistrates considerable time should be devoted to experimental studies in the psychology of examining witnesses; and in the matter of promoting a judge to a higher rank the patient penetration with which he succeeds in deciphering the cryptograms hidden in the hearts of the witnesses should count more than the intelligence he displays in reading the printed codes.

❖

SOMETIMES the emphasis which both judges and lawyers place on questions of law or questions of fact is determined less by the necessities of the case than by tactical considerations that the experts discover in reading between the lines of the decision.

Under the old French system, when the jurisdiction of the *parlements* allowed appeals for error in fact but not for error in law, the consummate lawyer succeeded in disguising every legal question as one of fact, but the lawyers of today who appear before the Court of Cassation, which reviews only questions of law, find pretexts in the most modest and concrete factual circumstances for disputing *de apicibus iuris*.

But I wish that the trial judges would not have recourse to this lawyer's expedient! It is painful to see a judge industriously overlook an essential question of law and hand down a decision based exclusively on the facts as if to cover his judgment with thick armor to withstand not only the blows of the lawyers (and this may well be a blessing!), but also the penetrating eyes of the supreme court (and this doubtless is an evil).

❖

To say of a judge that his decisions are fine in the sense that they are exquisite essays, exposing a dazzling erudition, is not to my way of thinking a way to compliment him. Decisions should simply be just, within the limits of human possibility. If we bear in mind the seriousness of the function they are supposed to perform, which is that of bringing peace to men, we cannot evaluate opinions on purely esthetic criteria unless we hold that justice can be reduced to the level of a literary diversion or a schoolboy's theme.

Nor should it be forgotten that if style is to be prized above all else in opinions, credit for their excellence should be given to the lawyers, since many of the stylistic gems which adorn the judge's opinions are culled from the lawyer's briefs. But the conscientious judge knows that whereas it may be proper for him to borrow rhetorical ornaments and erudition from the lawyer in order to make his dialectical premises more brilliant, when the time comes to render judgment, he must forget literature and search within himself for the unadorned word of justice which, disdainful of beautiful phrases, is most appropriately expressed in monosyllables.

CHAPTER X

On Sentiment and Logic in Judicial Decisions

WRITTEN opinions are an aid to justice when they reproduce in the manner of the topographical sketch the logical itinerary which the judge has traveled in reaching
his destination. In such cases, if the conclusion is erroneous, it is a simple matter to trace his reasoning back
to the point where he lost his way.

But how often is the written opinion a faithful repro-
duction of the judge's train of thought? How often is
the judge in a position to disclose even to himself the
motives which have led him to his decision?

The decision is thought of as the result of a purely
logical process, coldly considered in the abstract, bound
together by an inexorable chain of premises and conclusions. But in reality under all the trappings of magis-
tracy the judges are only human beings through whom
invisible magnetic forces are playing, forces which at-
tract and repel them, humanly and illogically, toward
certain conclusions and away from others. How can an
opinion faithfully reproduce the judge's motives if it
fails to take into consideration the subterranean mean-
derings of these sentimental currents from whose influence even the most austere judge is never free?

❖

ALTHOUGH one still hears it said that an opinion can be
reduced to a syllogism, that it is based on premises from
which conclusions are logically derived, it frequently
happens in practice that the judge reverses the procedure by working backwards from conclusions to premises. The Italian judge is encouraged to follow this

reverse order by the procedure which requires him to an-
nounce his decision at the close of the hearings, but gives
him a few days of grace for writing the opinion. The law
seems to suggest that the judge's difficulty lies less in
rendering a decision than in substantiating it.

In spite of its name, then, the thesis frequently pre-
cedes the hypothesis; the roof is built before the walls. I
do not suggest, however, that the judgment is reached
blindly and that the opinion is merely an exercise in
mental gymnastics, to make the judgment appear the
result of rigorous logic when actually it was arrived at
in a purely arbitrary manner; I merely point out that
sentiment and intuition play a larger part in judicial
"reasoning" than is apparent to the layman. It is not for
nothing that the word "decision" (*sentenza*) is derived
from the word "to feel" (*sentire*).

❖

In order to show the psychological difference between the
lawyer and the judge, it has been said that the former
starts from the conclusion that his client is right and
proceeds to prove the premises which would lead to that
conclusion; while the latter examines the premises presented to him in the hearings and derives a conclusion
from them which forms the basis of his judgment.

But in practice the distinction is not always so clear.
Sometimes the judge too is working backwards, trying
logically to rationalize a decision which he has already
reached by sentiment. Both lawyer and judge, then, may
anticipate the conclusion. In the case of the lawyer, the
conclusion is presented to him by his client; in the case
of the judge, by a mysterious and clairvoyant intuition
which is called a sense of justice.

GOOD judges rely more on their moral sensibilities than on any dialectical virtuosity; and when they are constrained to fill their opinions with high-sounding legal phrases, they consider this task a luxury to be indulged by temporarily unemployed intellectuals, because they are convinced that whatever their inner voice dictates has little need of rational apology.

❖

ALL lawyers know that there are many more correct decisions than there are irrefutable supporting arguments, for many times after the Court of Cassation has remanded a case for a new trial on the grounds of poor reasoning, the lower court has felt impelled to reach the same decision, backing it with a more careful opinion. This happens because there are judges whose moral sensibilities are greater than their intellectual prowess, who intuitively grasp the just solution of the conflict although they lack the dialectical agility necessary to demonstrate it.

I believe the most agonizing predicament for a scrupulous judge must be to have his conscience tell him the just solution of a case, and to be unable to seize upon the argument which will substantiate it. At such times the judge needs a little of the lawyer's talent, since his opinion is like a brief for the position his conscience bids him defend.

❖

IN the hope of seeing their "brilliant" opinions published in the law reports or having them create favorable impressions when promotion is being considered, there is a danger that some judges will treat the decision as the point of departure for a brilliant essay rather than a bridge of passage to the just conclusion—the true function of the judicial process. The judge who is intent only upon presenting casual readers with the delight of a literary masterpiece, instead of offering a just solution to the suffering of the parties, fails to comprehend the holy function of justice. He is the judicial counterpart of the legendary Padre Zappata, the priest who reasoned well but preached badly.

❖

A just decision is not always well reasoned, and conversely a well reasoned decision is not always just. Sometimes a summary opinion is an indication that the judge was so certain of the correctness of his decision that he considered a careful and detailed opinion superfluous. On the other hand, a careful and detailed opinion may indicate a desire on the part of the judge to conceal his perplexity from himself or others by means of logical arabesques.

❖

It has been said that too much intelligence is harmful to a judge, but I do not subscribe to this. I do say, however, that the best judge is the one in whom a ready humanity prevails over cautious intellectualism. A sense of justice, the innate quality bearing no relation to acquired legal techniques, which enables the judge after hearing the facts to feel which party is right, is as necessary to him as a good ear is to a musician; for, if this quality is wanting, no degree of intellectual pre-eminence will afford adequate compensation.

CHAPTER XI

On the Lawyer's Love for the Judge and Vice Versa

PAY no attention to the lawyer who, having lost a case, vents his anger and disappointment on the judges, pretending to scorn them and hate them. His humor is as fleeting as lovers' jealousies; the heart of the lawyer belongs to the court, the cross and joy of his life.

If revelers, returning from the theater late at night, pass under the lawyer's window, they will find it illuminated; if they look in, they will see him at his desk in the quiet of the night, composing love letters to his lady, who is also being pressed by a rival—letters ardent, prolix, emphatic, boresome, like all of their kind—but the lawyer's letters are briefs, and the lawyer's mistress is the court.

If you find a lawyer in a library scanning the stacks for dusty tomes which no one else ever reads, you may know that he is seeking the magic formulae discovered by hoary wizards long ago which will teach him how to enchant the lady of his heart—the court.

And if, some Sunday afternoon, the lawyer takes a solitary stroll in the country, do not think that he merely whiles away his time; follow him and you will find that when he believes he is alone at last his face will light up as if inspired, he will begin to gesticulate and, turning to the trees, the habitual confidants of lovers, will repeat in sweet accents the phrases of his eternal passion: "May it please the Honorable Court."

❖

IT is said that lawyers do not hold judges in the degree of honor that they merit. Nevertheless, I know certain lawyers who, eager to move the judges more deeply by the harmony of their tones, by the grace of their gestures, and by the suavity of their smiles, memorize their long addresses and practice them before a mirror. What lover reaches such extremes of devotion that he stands before a mirror rehearsing the well-turned phrases that will make his mistress yield?

✧

A young lawyer, who still had the enthusiasm of the neophyte, once asked this question: "I have tried three cases. Twice I was sure my client was right. I spent long weeks preparing my briefs, setting forth my case elaborately and eloquently. In the other instance I was afraid my client was in the wrong, so I wrote only a few lines proposing oral testimony. I lost the former cases and won the latter. Now, how should I act in the future?"

An old, experienced lawyer replied: "You should study each case thoroughly, seeking to discover the best and most convincing defense, but you should not forget to prepare the usual procedural objections as well. These latter should never be substituted for the more serious grounds, but should flank them, as it were. Thus, if you should appear before a competent judge, as will generally happen, he will decide in your favor on the merits of the case, but if you find yourself pleading before a superficial magistrate you will win the case on the other grounds."

✧

If in writing his decision a judge speaks of one of the attorneys as "able" or "learned," it is usually done to soften the blows which are to follow. That is, it is generally an indication that the court has been neither swayed by his ability nor convinced by his learning.

If in reading a long-awaited decision a lawyer comes
across any such laudatory epithets addressed to him, he
need read no further, being already assured that he has
lost the case.

✧

WHEN the layman in the courtroom tries to guess the
outcome of a case by scrutinizing the attitude of the
judges, he is almost certain to come to the wrong conclusion. If the judges listen to an attorney with great attention, this is no indication, as the layman might believe,
that they are in agreement with him. Rather it is a sign
that, being of the opposite opinion, they are curious to
hear what arguments he will employ in support of a position which they have already decided is untenable. But if
the court pays little attention to a lawyer and asks him
to conclude briefly, this in turn is no indication that he
has lost the case; it may only show that the court does
not like to waste time hearing arguments of which they
have already silently approved.

The young lawyer should learn to rejoice when the
judge interrupts him in court. But he should also learn
to fear the friendly smile of the judge whom he meets on
the street; for after having decided a case against a lawyer, judges are disposed to pay him small courtesies to
show that they bear him no personal animosity.

✧

WHEN you have lost a case, young lawyer, I counsel you
to go to the court files and look carefully through your
briefs. Often you will find comments scribbled in the margins by the judges, and these will point out far better
than the formal opinion wherein lay the weaknesses of
your case. Even if you do not find any open reprobation,
certain underlinings, certain marks of approval, will

faithfully reveal the judge's estimation of your ability, and this will serve as a useful guide for the future.

Conversely, do not put down your own impressions on the margins of the decision, for tomorrow it may fall into the hands of the judge who wrote it.

✧

Contrary to the layman's belief, personal friendship between the judge and the lawyer is not an advantage to the client; for a scrupulous judge is so afraid that he will unconsciously favor his friend that in reaction he tends to be unjust to him.

When an honest judge must decide a case between a friend and someone he does not know, he finds it more difficult to decide in favor of the friend than against him, for greater courage is needed to risk the appearance of injustice in an attempt to be just than to be unjust in order to save the appearances of justice.

CHAPTER XII

*On the Sorrows and Sacrifices in the
Life of the Judge*

IN Plato's *Republic* judges and doctors are treated with
a similar diffidence, as if the necessity of their presence
were an indication of the physical or moral sickness of
the citizens.

This psychological affinity between the two professions is no less evident today, particularly because of
that common feeling of compassion which daily prox-
imity with another's ills, either physical or moral, awak-
ens in the man who must watch and comfort him. Judges
and doctors alike are surrounded by the leprous and the
deformed. All their lives judges breathe the fetid air of
diseased places, of those gray hospitals of human cor-
ruption, the courtrooms.

❖

I know of a chemist who occasionally distills poisons in
his laboratory. Then he wakens with a start in the night
remembering with terror that a milligram of that substance would suffice to kill a man. How then can a judge
sleep tranquilly when he knows that he has in a secret
chest that subtle poison which is called injustice, one
drop of which escaping through mischance may not only
take life, but, more terrible still, may give to life a bitter
destructive flavor which no kindness can ever remove?

❖

THE good judge takes equal pains with every case no
matter how humble; he knows that important cases and
unimportant cases do not exist, for injustice is not one
of those poisons which, though harmful when taken in

large doses, yet when taken in small doses may produce a salutary effect. Injustice is a dangerous poison even in doses of homeopathic proportions.

❖

JUST as to divert themselves with exciting adventures, far removed from the monotonous routine of daily existence, the middle classes like to read detective stories or to see lurid melodramas, so the judge seeks in the theater or in novels happenings which contrast sharply with his daily experience. He likes pictures of loving spouses superimposed on pink and blue backgrounds, brothers who amicably divide their inheritance, merchants who do not go bankrupt, and landowners who meet on their common boundary to express with tears in their eyes their mutual joy at being neighbors.

❖

THE judge is denied the hour of spiritual relaxation which other men may find in the conversation of friends at mealtime, for the law which forbids him to dine regularly with a person who may appear before him, compels him to take his repasts in ascetic solitude.

The young graduate should bear this in mind and consider carefully whether he has found his true vocation before entering on a legal career, for during his novitiate, perhaps even before he is married, he will be assigned as the local judge in some provincial town where his table in the only restaurant must be set apart and where he must eat his meals in silence. The sole companion admitted there is invisible but ever present—his independence.

❖

IN certain cities of the Netherlands the cutters of precious stones live in obscure little shops. All day they weigh on their scales jewels so rare that one alone would suffice to lift them forever from their poverty. But every evening when they have reconsigned these sparkling gems to their eagerly awaiting owners, they appear serene, and on that same table where previously they had weighed another's treasure without sign of envy, they spread their frugal supper, and with the hands that had polished the diamonds of the rich they break the bread of their honest poverty.

Even thus lives the judge.

✧

I know of no office which requires of him who holds it a stronger sense of dignity than that of the judge—a sense which compels one to look into his own conscience rather than to the commands of others for the justification of his actions and to assume responsibility for them openly and fully.

The independence of judges, the principle which obliges them at the moment of handing down a decision to feel unfettered by any hierarchal subordination, is a hard privilege demanding of its possessor the courage to stand alone without hiding behind the convenient screen of another's authority.

For this reason the custom of the collegial court, which is often considered a guarantee of justice by the parties, was perhaps originally devised for the comfort of the judges, to give them companionship in the loneliness of their independence.

✧

In the heated discussions which arise from time to time between the protagonists of the collegial bench and of the single judge I heard one of the former school argue in this wise:

"I will even admit that judges may prefer the custom of the single judge because it flatters their pride and frees them from time-consuming deliberation in the judges' chambers, but I will not admit that lawyers favor this custom, for they are too well aware of the perils of first impressions untempered by the control of later discussion."

I suggest that this argument could better be reversed.

I think that lawyers prefer a single judge, for they know that when their clients are in the right it is easier to convince one man of this fact than to convince three, but I do not admit that judges prefer this custom, at least those who are still aware of the terror of being alone in the agony of judgment.

❖

IT is the judges rather than the lawyers who should be grateful to the complicated and slow-moving Italian procedure which seems to be made not so much for encumbering their work (as is often said), as for permitting their consciences to rest in peace. The fear of having pronounced an unjust decision might well be so disquieting to a conscientious judge as to keep him awake at night. But he knows that there is the right to appeal, and the comforting thought that his error is not without remedy aids him gently in falling asleep.

When a judge has not been able to reach a definite conclusion at the end of a case, he can free himself from this predicament by inviting one of the parties to take the decisary. Thus even if the party may perjure himself, the judge, by deciding in conformity with the oath, puts his own conscience at rest, as the blame for the possible injustice is transferred from him to the perjurer.

I feel a subtle uneasiness when I meet a retired magistrate who has decided to practice law coming to court with a brief case under his arm to ask for a continuance. Of course the bar and the bench are morally on the same level, and one does not lower himself in changing the robe of the judge for that of the lawyer. Still, only yesterday we saw him on the bench, austere and solemn, ready to censure our lawyer's squabbles, and we felt that he was superior to us because in exercising impartiality all his life he had reached that serene peace of mind which permits older men to evaluate and commiserate from above all the passions and desires of turbulent youth, as troubles which can no longer reach them. It is painful to see him now among us, panting and bitter in the midst of our struggles, and to hear his voice, tremulous with age, assume tones of rhetorical anger in behalf of his client.

There is no more pathetic spectacle than that of an elderly man adventuring on a style of youthful intemperance which, in order not to appear ludicrous, requires the spendthrift agility of a college student. Even for certain courtroom tactics, the spontaneity of youth is necessary; I have never felt the mortification of these expedients so strongly as when I have seen them practiced with ingenuous awkwardness by these old beginners who in the decline of their worthy lives try to learn to be partisan.

❖

THE true drama of the judge is not the one which now and then appears in novels and plays, and which generally deals with a violent struggle between his public duty and his private passions—as when the prosecuting attorney is unknowingly called upon to prosecute his own son, or better still, when the judge discovers that the crime he is investigating was committed by himself in a state of somnambulism. Much less exotic is the grief which feeds the daily drama of the judge.

This drama is loneliness; for in order to render judgment, the judge must be free from human bonds, he must be placed a step above his equals; at this level rarely does he find the affectionate friendship he desires, and if he sees it approaching he must be careful lest it be prompted only by the hope of his favors or lest it move him to betray his impartiality.

The drama of the judge is the daily contemplation of human sorrow and human weakness which fill his world. Here there is no place for the happy faces of those who live in peace, but only for the grieving distorted faces of those embroiled in litigation or vilified by guilt.

But above all, the drama of the judge is habit which, insidious as a disease, wears him down and discourages him so that finally he feels that passing on a man's life or his honor has become an ordinary act of administration.

The judge who becomes accustomed to rendering justice is like the priest who becomes accustomed to saying mass. Fortunate indeed is that country priest who, approaching the altar with senile step, feels the same sacred turbulation in his breast which he felt as a young priest at his first mass. And happy is that magistrate who even unto the day of his retirement experiences the same religious exaltation in rendering judgment which made him tremble fifty years before, when as a young praetor he handed down his first decision.

An old magistrate, feeling that he was about to die, lying serenely on his bed, prayed in this fashion:

"O Lord, I would that all the men I have sentenced should die before me because I would fain not think of leaving men who were imprisoned on my order to suffer human punishment in the prisons of this world. When I shall appear before thy throne, O Lord, I would find them in spirit on the threshold to tell me that they know I judged them according to what men call justice, and if without knowing it I have been unjust toward any one, him more than any other I would meet there to beg his forgiveness and to tell him that not a single time in rendering judgment have I forgotten that I am a poor human creature, a slave of error, that not a single time in sentencing a man has my conscience not been disturbed, trembling before an office which ultimately can belong to none but thee, O Lord."

CHAPTER XIII

On the Sorrows and Sacrifices in the
Life of the Lawyer

IF some poor unknown accused, facing a difficult and
dangerous, long drawn-out trial, finds a lawyer willing
to treat him with kindness and to defend his case, it is
because cupidity and fame are not the only passions
harbored within the lawyer's heart; there is room, too,
for Christian charity which forbids us to leave the
innocent alone in his grief, or the guilty alone in his
shame. But there is also something finer in the heart
of the lawyer; for a man who sees the injustice with
which the law sometimes threatens the innocent, and,
instead of hastening on pretending not to have seen,
stops and shakes his fist in the face of overbearing
authority, and careless of his own peril generously
throws himself into the struggle on the side of the
oppressed—this is called Civil courage, a virtue still
more rare than charity.

Let this be remembered by those who seem eager
to quip the lawyers on their proverbial rapacity.

❖

I watched an old lawyer standing at the entrance of one
of the courtrooms in the Palazzo di Giustizia, dressed
in his toga, awaiting his case. A tired and strained look
was on his face as he leaned against the door with his
eyes cast down in an almost ecstatic contemplation of his
hands, which were clasped together as in prayer. He
seemed wrapped in silence as he stood there amid
the comings and goings of his noisy and busy colleagues. But on approaching I discovered that it was

not prayer which engrossed him; his eyes were fixed on his wrist-watch as he was intently counting his pulse.

Suddenly he was aroused from his reverie by an indiscreet colleague who fatuously asked him whether he was ill. As if awakened from a dream he answered in a dull voice, "The doctor says that people with heart trouble should not try cases."

Only then did I notice the pallor of his brow. Under the wax-colored skin covering his temples I saw the winding course of those little veins, the appearance of which is considered by the superstitious a sign of an imminent death. Just then the usher called his case, and he disappeared into the courtroom. When I entered soon after I was aghast to see this same bent suffering man transformed into a robust orator, warming to the discussion, prodigiously alive, gesticulating vehemently with the very arm with which only a few minutes before he had been fearfully taking his pulse.

Now that the victory of his client was at stake, he never thought of restraining his gestures or of moderating his excited delivery, which alone was enough to burst one of those fragile little arteries and start him on his last voyage.

❖

THE highest form of charity does not consist in giving material aid to some unfortunate and then quickly leaving him to his grief with no more thought for him; the charitable man should not so betray his haste to forget the troubles of one he has befriended; he must patiently give ear to the tales of another's misery, comfort him by sharing his grief and sympathizing with his lot. He who can make a suffering man believe that the story of his troubles is the object of sympathetic personal concern to the listener relieves him of that horrible sense of loneliness in the face of pain which the sick struggle to overcome by repeating to the doctor over and over again every detail of their symptoms.

Lawyers like doctors practice daily that rite of social solidarity which consists in consoling persons who are face to face with pain, and for this reason the liberal professions of medicine and law have rightly been called charitable professions. Just as the patient likes to confide his troubles to the doctor even if he has given up hope of getting well, the client, even when he is resigned to losing his case, seeks out a lawyer in order to find some person willing to hear step by step the story of his personal troubles, which seem as big as the world to their bearer, but which to any listener other than the lawyer seem a sordid chain of unsavory occurrences.

It is commonly believed that the specific function of the lawyer is to persuade the judge to listen to him. His most charitable function, however, is to listen to his client, giving him the solace of knowing he has at least one tireless confidant who will hear his troubles. In leaving the office of these lay confessors, the client feels freed and purified; he is aware that the most acute part of his pain has magically been imprisoned and tamed in the lawyer's notebook. A beneficial chemical reaction has occurred by means of which that subtle poison, anger, which circulates through the blood, is transformed into a neutral substance no longer burning the lips. All this is the work of the lawyer, that accomplished pharmacist of the passions.

WHEN a client first enters my office, he is by definition a bore. If he could read my heart at that time he would flee from me, horrified by my opinion of him. Then, repressing my first impulse to rebel, I attempt a smile and ask him to be seated, sighing inwardly at the cruel fate of the lawyer, to whom society has given the rare privilege of serving as lightning rods to trouble-makers, drawing them into his office and making them gently unburden themselves in this isolation ward protected by piles of dusty papers, so that they will not imperil the tranquility of the rest of the world by exploding in public.

The client takes a seat before me and with the resignation of a victim prepared for the sacrifice I ask his business. For the first few minutes I am unable to pay attention to what he is saying; stimulated by the strange voice of this intruder who speaks of notes overdue, or of goods not up to specification, my thoughts are seeking to travel to imaginary shores where neither notes nor goods exist, and that bore who insists on telling me his personal troubles (where do I come in, what are his personal worries to me who barely know him?) becomes confused in my mind with the man who seizes me by the coat sleeves and prevents me from leaping into the boat which is just putting out to sea.

But as the client's story unfolds, gradually, almost without being aware of it, I begin to pay attention. At first it is the exterior aspects of the client which arouse my curiosity—his physiognomy, his clothes, his gestures; then I begin to notice the accent, the pauses and the turns of the sentences which perhaps reveal hesitations, or tortuosities of thought. Frequently I catch myself counting the number of therefores or howevers he uses. Thus, slowly, I am recalled to my profession. Some sentence he utters becomes the point of departure for a first diagnosis, as the categories of human ills are so few in number basically that it does not take much time or thought to make a rough classification. Then I begin to see the individual case shaping itself within the broad general characteristics of the type. I notice that there is some chapter in the story upon which the client touches lightly or is silent, some fact or series of facts he seeks with trepidation to circumvent. Beneath these hesitating phrases I discover some shame he does not want to confess, a bitterness he wishes to forget, almost as if he feared to open some old wound which pained him still. Then I see that the abstract classification no longer fits; it is necessary to leave behind that generic professional indifference which treats generalities, and with a respectful desire of comprehension to approach the individual case which is unlike any other, for every human being is unique and every grief is new.

At this point I must interrupt my client, bringing him back to the point, asking him to clarify those parts of his story which he has skipped over. Gradually my questioning brings together the fragments of his narrative, co-ordinating and uniting them into a whole. We have changed positions, now. Before he had bored me with his story. Now I embarrass him with my questions. And when I finally let him rest, he has unburdened his heart, and his case is mine. I know his problems better than he, for they have been transcribed in an ordered and clarified form in my mind and there have assumed a logic which was lacking before. And if he would know how this has happened, it would be his turn to ask questions of me.

When the client leaves, the world of the lawyer is enriched with a new experience or, rather, a new pain, but also with an added reason for having an affectionate feeling toward life. The client who entered as a bore was found underneath to be a weak man in need of advice and encouragement, an innocent man in need of legal aid, or perhaps a friend in need of consolation. Thus the lawyer sits alone in his office caressing his trusted codes, his mind no longer yearning for escape to the blue sea; he must remain on land, where there is work to be done.

❖

THOSE who foolishly continue to describe lawyers as the vampires of their clients do not know of a certain Florentine lawyer who died in the prime of his career. To his colleagues who were with him during his last days, his life was almost symbolic of his profession.

In the first days of his illness, he would not admit even to himself that he had a fever, and he obstinately continued his customary routine of relentless, pitiless labor, his days all taken up with monotonous hearings and conferences with clients, and his nights until dawn spent preparing page after page of briefs in the silence of his library. But the strain of overwork had undermined his vigorous constitution, sapping his resistance, and the fever soon was too much for him. With shame and rebellion in his heart, he finally had to give up and go to bed, doggedly insisting, however, that it was nothing serious and that the next day he would be back at the office. He never left that bed again; for several days he struggled, demanding that the papers on his most important cases be brought him from his study, and insisting on going over them propped up in bed, but when his eyes and his mind finally rebelled he cried like a baby before his family at this prolonged illness which kept him from

his work, and he tormented his doctor, explaining over
and over again that lawyers could not afford to be sick.
"Bother with medicine! My clients' interests are at
stake—time limits are expiring."

As he grew worse the thought of cases which were coming up became an obsession. Sometimes, in a sort of reasoning delirium, he dictated disconnected sequences of
juridical argumentation, or addressed the judges as if
they were seated at the foot of his bed listening to him.
Later all his anxiety centered in one case, an appeal
before the Court of Cassation which was coming up soon,
and for which he was unwilling to request a delay, saying
a postponement would be a disgrace, repeating over and
over with that obstinacy of the sick with a fixed idea, "A
disgrace, a disgrace." In his last days he asked the doctors for nothing but to be made well before that case
came up, as if it were in their power to grant it, saying
that it was absolutely necessary that he leave for Rome
on that day to appear in court. In his feverish mind that
particular trial took on a fatal importance not only for
his client but for his own destiny as well. "If I can't take
part in that trial, I'm finished; if I don't win that case,
it means I can't get well."

And when every hope of recovery vanished, his friends
resolved on a pious deceit to keep him content. Without
his knowledge they arranged for a long postponement of
the hearing, and then on the day that the case would
have been heard, since notice of the postponement would
have seemed to him a bad augury, they had a telegram
sent from Rome, saying that the appeal had been fully
accepted, without the necessity for any hearing at all.
The telegram arrived when he was dying, but when it was
read to him, he opened his eyes for a moment and smiled,

murmuring, "Then I shall get well." These were his last words, and this was perhaps his last thought. His wife and children and a colleague or so from his office were at his bedside, but his last smile was for that telegram, for that announcement of justice which in his feverish mind was confused with the idea of getting well.

Perhaps he died without realizing it, at peace with himself for not having failed in his duty and not having compromised with this inopportune and unfortunate illness that which alone counted in his conscience—the victory of his client, who had come to him for the defense of his rights.

This man was neither a hero nor a saint; he was merely a lawyer.

CHAPTER XIV

On the Common Destiny of Judge and Lawyer

THE LAWYER: Blest art thou, O Judge, who canst proceed in thy work according to the even rhythm of an office routine, surrounded by the respectful quiet of the courtroom or the silent seclusion of thy chambers. For when the judge enters, every murmur is hushed. Far from the tumult is thy task done, where haste and confusion are not found; to thee is unknown the anxious tension of improvising and of eleventh-hour changes. No need hast thou to toil in search of arguments; we lawyers perform the heavy task of bringing them forth and it is for thee only to judge those arguments which we present thee; and better to meditate upon thy choice art thou provided with a cushioned bench, so that while other men sit to rest themselves, when seated thou art deemed at thy greatest work. But the toil of the lawyer knows neither schedule nor truth, for him every process opens another road that he must travel, every client presents another enigma that he must solve. The lawyer must be in a hundred places at one time, as his mind must ever follow a hundred scents. Even the hours of night are not for his pleasure or rest, for these also his clients claim, since it is then perhaps that he will carefully build them the impenetrable argument. In body and in spirit he is the ever watchful guardian as thou, O Judge, art Olympian repose, calmly awaiting.

❖

THE JUDGE: But thou knowest not, O Lawyer, what waves of questions, what storms of doubt are loosed beneath the outward calm of the seated magistrate. If often at night thou art awakened by the petulance of some churlish client, more often still my sleepless heart hammers out till dawn the agony of my indecision. What judge can sleep on the eve of a death sentence? And ever after the weight of that sentence is borne by the judge alone; the fear of mistake, the painful thought of innocence enchained bends him with heavy care. Judges no longer know how to laugh for, like masks, their faces bear the scars of a battle between mercy and justice. When thou hast presented thy client's case, thy task is done, O Lawyer, and thou canst then go free before the world, but although a judge may be given impassibility, he may never again know serenity.

❖

THE LAWYER: And thinkest thou the lawyer is serene? Seest thou not from thy high bench how he becomes white and worn before his time and how death comes precipitously upon him? The lawyer lives a hundred lives in one, the cares of a hundred different destinies are weighted upon his shoulders. And if for one brief week he betakes himself to the crest of a mountain or the tiller of a sloop, even unto these carefree places he may find no rest, for the hopes and the fears and the petty misery of the clients he sought to leave behind creep forth to seek him out. Mayhap he cares not for money himself, still must he sweat in the defense of another's money; be he of ever so immaculate honor, still he is bereft of the sleep of an honest man, and if he be so much a lover of peace that he would rather see himself robbed by his own servants than to trouble himself and them with accusations, still he must poison his very existence in mean efforts to save other people's pennies from the hands of their servants.

And when thou speakest of the anxiety of judgment,

thou who dost not bear in mind the torment of the lawyer, who knows, or at least believes, that thy judgment is in good part motivated by his ability. It is he who must find the argument which will sway thee; and if thou art guilty of a blunder his is the fault, for not having drawn thee in time from the path of error. No one can describe the agony of the lawyer who knows his client's innocence and yet fails to prove it, who finds himself unequal and powerless before the ability and perhaps the scheming of an adversary, and who after the final defeat too late comes upon that argument with which justice would have triumphed.

❖

THE JUDGE: I understand, but still shouldst thou not consider the prize which is the lawyer's who brings his client victory? Through all the proceeding he is the center of attention and sympathy, the public shares his heart beats; it is lifted by his eloquence. While in the back of the hall the passive silent judge is like unto a useless scenic decoration and if in the end the truth does triumph, the praise is not for the judge who has distilled it from the tumult in his heart; it is for the lawyer, who appears as the champion of justice and who receives, not the dark torment of the judge, but glory and riches.

❖

THE LAWYER: Speak not of riches. Thou knowest well that the true lawyer, he who devotes his life to his high profession, will ever die poor. Only those become rich who under the mantle of the bar cloak merchants' and traders' hearts, like certain glib specialists in divorce. And as for glory and the gratitude of clients, be thou grateful, O Judge, that the lawyer stands between you and his clients, and saves you from looking into their faces. Thy world is found in the polished language of the lawyer, who has removed the dross of sordid reality from the lives and deeds of his clients and has brought before thee the quintessence in legal terminology. The arrogance of litigants, their folly and their villainy, is removed in the lawyer's office before a case reaches court. It is the lawyer who sterilizes the dispute in the light of the codes and of grammar and gallantry as well. He clarifies and cleanses reality. He washes the facts, removes from them the filth in which they have existed, and with a polite inclination places them, cleaned and isolated, on thy table.

But in this dour labor of disinfecting, do not believe that the lawyer is comforted by the gratitude of those who come to him for aid, for if he dares courteously to suggest that the lawyer is not meant to serve as a screen for lies, the client takes offense; if he counsels him to refrain from instituting a foolish suit the client thinks him pusillanimous; if he says that in order not to annoy the court one must be simple and direct in speech and writing, the client deems him lazy. When the lawyer is successful, after no one can say what pain and travail, and wins a desperate case, the client lets him know that the victory was due less to the lawyer's prowess than to a word from a friend of the family who, unknown to the lawyer, had intervened at the last minute. When the lawyer loses, the client is certain that he has let himself be bribed by the opposing advocate; when he requests a delay because the judge is taking his holidays, the fault is still the lawyer's who in prolonging the case hopes to charge a higher fee. And let us not talk of the pitiless selfishness of the client who forgets that even a lawyer's strength has limits, that he too is a man who knows fatigue and illness. If to a client who is for the twentieth time explaining his plight one says, with a pallid smile, that one has a fever and can listen no longer, he will stare with uncomprehending astonishment, and then continue his story, for he deems it the lawyer's duty to be interested in his private affairs, while never condescending to interest himself in those of the lawyer.

✧

THE JUDGE: But even the office of judge is a pitiless one, and thou also, O Lawyer, art often pitiless against us. It happens sometimes that in the heart of the seated magistrate throb all the passions of grieving humanity—the agony of betrayed love, the anxiety of a dying child. But these voices must be silenced in the courtroom; the heart of the judge must be unencumbered even when his deepest, most secret emotions are moved. Even if the man feels that the question he is deciding is of a hundred times less moment than his grief, the judge must deem this grief a minor thing to the case, no matter how futile, which he is called upon to decide; and while the man sobs, thinking of the son who died just yesterday, the magistrate must listen to the defending attorney who for three hours mercilessly explains why the tenant failed to pay his rent.

✧

THE LAWYER: Thou accuseth the lawyer of not taking pity upon you, as if he were speaking for his own pleasure. Canst thou not conceive the lawyer's pain when, certain that he is defending justice, he speaks but to convince the judge and knows that he is failing, and who desperately continues to speak though his strength declines, under the all-consuming urge to add something more, to give all for the triumph of truth? Hast thou not seen the attorney pale as he spoke and put his hand for a moment on his heart in a sudden gesture of pain which is quickly lost in the stream of his discourse?

And then, if death does not take him at the height of his career, slowly with old age there comes a lonely solitude. Even clients follow the fashion and prefer the self-assured audacity of youth to the tremulous wisdom of age. And the old men sit alone in their dusty offices which no one ever visits, and during the long hours of idleness their eyes wander slowly over the cases filled with half a century's accumulation of legal papers which on some not distant day their nephews will throw away unopened.

✧

THE JUDGE: But more lonely still is the retired magistrate, despoiled of his gold and emerald, an exiled idle old man who seeks a little sun in the public parks and passes his days recalling the group of devoted friends he had about him on the bench now suddenly scattered and dispersed by the inexorable law of retirement. And even more profound and pathetic is the loneliness of these old beginners who, seeking to round out their meager pension and to linger within the accustomed halls, attempt to practice law, only to become lost in the crowd of young lawyers.

✧

THE LAWYER: This is our life, O Judge, and if it is given to us to grow old, this in the end will be our fate. And yet I know I would at no cost alter my destiny.

✧

THE JUDGE: Nor I; for it seems to me that among the professions that mankind can serve no other is better suited to maintain peace among men than that of the judge, the dispenser of a balm for every wound, called justice. For this, even though the end of my life seem lonely, it will be sweet and serene, for I know that the knowledge of having spent the better part of myself to bring about the just happiness of others will give me peace and hope at the end.

In this hope, O Lawyer, our destinies meet at their terrestrial conclusion. We are brothers in this common purpose and therefore can shake hands.